Instructor's Manual
to accompany

Readings
for Writers

eighth edition

Jo Ray McCuen
Glendale College

Anthony Winkler

Harcourt Brace College Publishers
Fort Worth   Philadelphia   San Diego   New York   Orlando   Austin   San Antonio
Toronto   Montreal   London   Sydney   Toyko

Address for editorial correspondence:
Harcourt Brace College Publishers
301 Commerce St. Suite 3700,
 Fort Worth, Texas 76102

Address for Orders:
Harcourt Brace and Company,
6277 Sea Harbor Drive
Orlando, Fl 32887-6777
1-800-782-4479
1-800-433-0001 (in Florida)

ISBN: 0-15-502170-2

Printed in the United States of America
4 5 6 7 8 9 0 1 2 3 051 0 9 8 7 6 5 4 3 2 1

Table of Contents

Chapter Four: Planning and Organizing

Chapter Five: Developing Paragraphs

Chapter Six: Reporting: Narration, Description, Process

Chapter Seven: Explaining: Illustration and Definition

Chapter Eight: Analyzing: Comparison/Contrast, Division/Classification, and Causal Analysis

Chapter Nine: Argumentation

Chapter Ten: The Meaning of Words

CORRELATION CHART

between

READINGS FOR WRITERS, eighth edition

and

HARBRACE COLLEGE HANDBOOK, twelfth edition

READINGS FOR WRITERS	HARBRACE HANDBOOK
Chapter 1	G-33
Chapter 2	29d, 27a, G-36
Chapter 3	19b-19c, 19g, 19i, 33a G-39, 33d
Chapter 4	32b, 33e, 29a-c
Chapter 5	32
Chapter 6	32d
Chapter 7	32c, 32d(7)
Chapter 8	32d
Chapter 9	31
Chapter 10	19, 20

Chapter One DEFINING RHETORIC

Tilly Warnock *How I Write* (pp. 7-16)

Answers to Questions About the Facts

1. Her "golden dream" was to have a book dedicated to her, to inspire a book rather than write one of her own.
2. The term "rat in the basement," ascribed by the author to her colleague, Fred Homer, refers to Writing fears, or secret fears that stifle the urge to write. Allow open discussion of the second half of the question, which asks students to describe their own personal rats.
3. He said he never gets writer's block; he just lowers his standards.
4. The terms are "gushers" and "eekers" and refer to writers who either erupt explosively on the page or whose work seeps out sentence by sentence. Allow open discussion of the second half of the question.
5. When you're doing the dishes.

Answers to Questions About the Strategies

1. Her style is conspicuously down-to-earth, graceful, and easy-going, almost with the ease and flow of journeyman magazine writing. She avoids jargon and occasionally uses words and quotations one would not expect from the pen of an English teacher; for example, the quotation from Hemingway about the indispensability to a writer of a "built-in-shock-proof shit-detector. " Point these virtues out to students if only to demonstrate that English teachers do not always write with cant and jargon.
2. The author opens with an anecdote that sketches the indignant reaction of a participant in a fireplace conversation who bristled when asked about including collaboration as a stage in the writing process. She then moves to the frank admission that, contrary to the unidentified writer's opinions, no words she writes are hers and that she never writes alone. This theme of never writing alone is important to the structure of her article and is, in fact, the one on which she ends her discussion: "I am also fairly certain that I will never learn to write but that I will continue learning, with the help of others." The structure of the article, beginning and ending on the same theme, is circular.
3. These questions are not merely rhetorical, but have a structural purpose. She uses them to touch on upcoming topics and smooth the transition to them.

4. She ends both paragraphs with the same transition question, "What else helps?" There is enough material intruding between the use of these identical transitions for it not to be noticed except by picky editors such as these writers.
5. She uses herself and her experience as a writer as a primary source of supporting details, as well as the experiences of her students. She also cites the testimony of many other writers, from William Stafford to Donald Murray. Her details are quite effective, although they strike us as being more revealing of what she fears about writing than of how she actually writes.

Answers to Questions About the Issues

1. It is, of course, the author's job to be self-conscious and scrutinizing about writing techniques, but we are occasionally struck by her self consciousness and wonder whether such dispassionate and minute self-scrutiny might not add to and worsen one's fears about writing rather than alleviate them. Ask your students how they feel.
2. Allow for open discussion.
3. To us it seems as if most of what the author says applies more to fiction or creative writing than to the sort of everyday expository writing students are asked to do. We find it, for example, a little silly to think that anyone having to write a factual report would have to sit by the window, pen poised in hand, waiting for the Muse's whispers. Allow for open discussion of the second part of the question.
4. This question asks for personal opinion. Allow for open discussion.
5. Allow for open discussion.

Martin Luther King, Jr. *I Have A Dream* (pp. 18-23)

Answers to Questions About the Facts

1. It is especially appropriate because the speech was being given at the Lincoln Memorial. Dr. King evokes Lincoln's spirit by opening his speech with a wording similar to the opening of the Gettysburg Address.
2. He says that the segregation and discrimination still exist and that blacks still languish in poverty.
3. He cautions them against bitterness and hatred and urges them to struggle on a high plane of dignity and discipline.
4. He urges an attitude of conciliation and moderation. In paragraph 12 he specifically warns his audience not to distrust all white people.

2

5. One can infer that blacks in the North are confined mainly to ghettos (paragraph 17), and that though blacks can vote in the North, they are effectively disenfranchised by having no candidates to vote for (paragraph 15).

Answers to Questions About the Strategies

1. Certainly one characteristic is its elevated style; another, its many religious allusions.
2. The analogy is that the Constitution and the Declaration of Independence were a promise of freedom and liberty to all Americans, a promissory note that the speaker says has "bounced."
3. Repetition.
4. The paragraphs of this speech are short, charged with emotion and memorable phrases, and lacking in conceptual content. The paragraphs of a writer are likely to be longer and to contain more specific details.
5. It is a transitional paragraph.

Answers to Questions About the Issues

1. In the United States, brown people are called black, sepia people are called black; in fact, people are called black who are certainly not black. Blackness here seems not to be a designation of color but purely a designation of race. A trivial point you may say, but not so. In the West Indies, for example, careful discriminations are made that accurately designate skin color. It is only here in the United States that black is used as a sweeping and absolute category. Some Southern statutes designate as "black" any individual who has even a fractional and distant black ancestry. This ought to make an interesting discussion, since we can think of no other instance where Americans are so careless with color designations (a person who called a brown car black would be hooted away as a fool). The point is that "black" in American-speak means something beyond mere color. Try and draw out of your students what it actually means.
2. Allow for open discussion. Ignorance is our candidate.
3. Ditto.
4. Black men are among the most discriminated-against class of citizens on the face of the earth. Black women seem not to bear as cruel and monstrous a load of rejection as their male counterparts. It may be that black men are seen by racists as a greater sexual threat than black women, but even so, we remain mystified by the obvious difference. Allow for open discussion.

5.   Allow for open discussion. Here's a little gem you might share with your class: "My discomfort at first in American theaters, however, was not because of what I saw but of what I smelled. . . . Among my own people I smelled a rank wild odor, not quite a stink, but certainly distressing and even alien to me at the time. . . . It was only a year or so of consuming American food, though still without milk to this day, that I was able to endure an evening among my own kind, and this is because I now smell like them." The writer is Pearl Buck, and the excerpt is taken from *My Several Worlds*, her autobiography. Her point? That when she first moved to the United States after living for forty years in China, she thought Americans smelled awful. Buck says that all Americans stink to Chinese noses, and she attributes the stench to American food.

John Keats *Letter to Fanny Brawne* (pp. 23-25)

Answers to Questions About the Facts

1.   The reason Keats gives for not writing sooner is that he has been surrounded by friends and hasn't had the opportunity to be alone to write.
2.   He says that he knew the very first week that he was her "vassal."
3.   He says he refuses to believe that there is anything about him to be admired.
4.   The two luxuries Keats says he has to brood over in his walks are Fanny's loveliness and the hour of his death.
5.   In this letter Keats says that he hates the world because it "batters too much the wings" of his self-will and expresses a desire to leave it.

Answers to Questions About the Strategies

1.   The love letter is an expression of intimacy to the beloved, and the main pressure on the writer is to give expression to the feelings of love in his or her heart. There is a terrible onus on the writer to be intimate, expressive, and eloquent, to find and express the literary equivalent of what he or she feels. None of this is easy. Implicit in this task are some consolations, however: under ordinary circumstances, the letter will be read by none but the beloved, and the writer is at least assured of privacy for his heart-rending mutterings. Second, the letter presumes an already profound and deep relationship between the writer and his beloved, whose existence—one hopes—would spur on the writer to the desired eloquence. Ask your students if they have ever written a love letter

and how the elements that entered into the writing differed from those that, say, enter into writing an essay for an examination.

2. It differs from a love letter today mainly in the level of formality. People of Keats's day were more formal and staid than we are today, and it showed even in their love making and expressions. Notice, for example, the high literary quality of the letter, and the use of words such as "vassal" and "manifested"—the latter striking us as oddly out of place among such fevered intimacy. Ask your students to reword particular sentences with a modern flavor and see what comes of the exercise.

3. The traditional role assumed by the man is one of supplicant and idolater of the woman, and the usual professions are of supplication and worship. Keats is well in line with this expected convention, as when he refers to himself as Fanny's "vassal" and speaks of praying to her star "like a Heathen." Ask your students if this same convention of self-effacing worship is expected of the man today when sits down to pen his beloved a love letter.

4. Frankly, we don't know. We can't imagine that a woman would go through the same fulminations of idolatry, but then—being squarely middle-aged—we aren't exactly up to date on modern love letter conventions in this feminist age. Ask your students about this.

5. The implication of the image in the last line of this letter casts Keats in the role of the idolater and Fanny, his beloved, in the role of the Goddess who is being worshipped.

Answers to Questions About the Issues

1. A modern psychologically-minded reader would most certainly diagnose Keats malaise of world-weariness as chronic depression and probably suggest therapy.

2. What might strike a reader as "purely poetical" in this letter is the extravagant longings as well as some of the phrasing such as "I tremble at domestic cares. . . ." For example, it is surely poetic hyperbole to write, "I have two luxuries to brood over in my walks, your Loveliness and the hour of my death." Ask your students to point to other sentences that suggests a heightened poetic sensibility.

3. Some of the common stereotypes in popular thought characterizes the poetic temperament as weak, indecisive, tremulous, impressionable, susceptible to influence, and generally alert and hypersensitive to beauty and the so-called "finer things." To show your students that all poets are not necessarily cut from the same cloth, bring a copy of one of Charles Bukowski's urban yawps into class and read it to the students.

5

4. Allow for open discussion as to whether or not any of the modern women in your class find anything offensive in this letter. One student pointed out to us that its tone was patronizing, especially in the salutation.

5. One of the questions Keats relegated to the postscript is some cryptic query about a dog named Bishop. From a purely literary standpoint, it is incongruous to wax poetic about one's "fair Star" and professing the desire to die at the lips of one's beloved while answering queries about a dog. That is no doubt why Keats decided to shunt the daily baggage of practical questions aside and deal with them separately in a postscript. The gesture tells us that even in writing his love letter, Keats was not merely pouring out his soul on paper, he was also making the effort to subsume the outpourings into some self-consciously shaped literary form.

Francis P. Church *Is There a Santa Claus?* (pp. 27-28)

Answers to Questions About the Facts

1. Answered in the first paragraph. Church says that Virginia's little friends "have been affected by the skepticism of a skeptical age."
2. See paragraph 2. With "love and generosity and devotion."
3. See paragraph 2. Church writes that without Santa Claus "There would be no childlike faith then, no poetry, no romance to make tolerable this existence. We should have no enjoyment, except in sense and sight. The eternal light with which childhood fills the world would be extinguished."
4. See paragraph 3. He writes that "The most real things in the world are those that neither children nor men can see."

Answers to Questions About the Strategies

1. The audience for this editorial is the little girl herself as well as the regular subscribers and readers of the *Sun*. Since editorials are written to reflect a collective opinion of the newspaper's editorial board, they tend to be written in high-flown language and with a touch of bombast. This one is not. It is written in plain and fairly simple language (note we include only one word in the vocabulary section) and with a direct and appealing style that an eight-year old might grasp with effort. Notice also the direct address to Virginia in paragraph 2 as well as the straightforward and simple sentence structure.
2. For the sake of answering the child's question, it was necessary for Church to assert plainly that there is a Santa Claus, which he does,

but for the sake of his adult readers who know better, he equates the concept of Santa Claus with all the bountiful gifts that the imagination bestows on our interpretation of the physical world. This dual meaning allows his editorial to answer the child while also addressing the adults.

3. It is a tone of mock-horror, the sort that adults often use at Christmas to playfully josh a doubting child.

4. "Fancy" as Church uses it in this sentence means "imagination." Nowadays it is only seldom used with that meaning.

Answers to Questions About the Issues

1 Some religious groups regard Christmas as strictly a religious holiday celebrating the birth of Christ, and consequently oppose Santa Claus on the grounds that he tends to secularize the holiday. As to whether or not this is a sound rationale or merely a kind of grumpiness, ask your students.

2. See our answer to question 1. Some say that Santa has commercialized the holiday by emphasizing gift-giving over religious reverence. Ask your students if they believe this.

3. Allow for open discussion. We can imagine the fire and fury that would spew forth from some *Sun* subscribers who are also parents of toddlers.

4. Some sourpusses have argued that a belief in Santa Claus causes eventual disillusionment in children when they find out the truth. Others say, as does Church, that belief in Santa Claus stimulates the imagination of children. Allow for the expression of opinion on this issue.

John Taylor *Are You Politically Correct?* (pp. 31-47)

Answers to Questions About the Facts

1. See paragraphs 5 and 6. According to the author, Baylin's crime was reading "from then diary of a southern planter without giving equal time to the recollections of a slave." Thernstrom, on the other hand, was charged with insensitively referring to Indians as "Indians" and with using the imperialist word "Oriental."

2. The author claims that the new fundamentalists are an eclectic collection of multiculturists, feminists, radical homosexuals, Marxists, and New Historicists, who are united "in the belief that Western culture and American society are thoroughly and hopelessly racist, sexist, oppressive."

7

3. See paragraph 16. The rationale used by the new fundamentalism in dismissing all dissent, according to Taylor, is the accusation of "false consciousness" that sees any dissenter as too steeped in "the oppressors' propaganda to see the truth."
4. See paragraphs 26 and 27. The author alleges that leftover student radicals from the 1960s are behind the emergence of the new fundamentalism of political correctness.
5. See paragraph 33. He claims that ethnic studies programs "now in place at most universities tend to divide humanity into five groups—whites, black, Native Americans, Hispanics, and Asians." He also adds that "homosexuals and feminists are usually included on the grounds that, through they are not a distinct ethnic group, they, too, have been oppressed by the 'whitemale'. . . .

Answers to Questions About the Strategies

1. The advantages of opening with taunts supposedly hurled at the beleaguered professor by students is immediate involvement of the reader in the story. The author ends his article on the same note by closing with similar epithets that were allegedly at another dean, this one at Yale, for suggesting that Western culture has produced tolerance and diversity.
2. In paragraphs 11 and 12 he likens the political correctness movement with the fundamentalism of the 1970s when Christian evangelists tried to suppress books and legislate their particular agenda on the school system. We question the fundamental fairness of this tactic, since it strikes us as somewhat specious to tar one movement with the brush of another. Ask your students what they think of it.
3. The author's case against the "new fundamentalism" consists primarily of statements he attributes to various players in the drama. For example, in paragraph 4, he cites a memo by an unidentified college administrator which inanely declares that the word *individual* is regarded as "racist." Yet he does not name the administrator nor the source of the memo. The weakness of his argument is this persistent lack of traceable sources and the use of hearsay testimony and unattributed statements. Ask your students to find other instances where the argument is weakened by this lack of a specific source. (See paragraph 21 for another example. What is the course book at the University of Texas that the author finds so riddled with illiterate writing?).
4. A scrupulous logician might make the objection that these are *ad hominem* arguments.

5. Argumentatively, it is a sound strategy to state the side of your opposition and then refute it. This article has a definite argumentative edge to it, and by outlining the justification for political correctness by its espousers, Taylor is then able to show what he considers the more sinister side of the movement.

Answers to Questions About the Issues

1. Allow for open discussion. The author is using this statement as an example of the radicalism that he states has begun to pervade our institutions. Ask your students their opinions of it.
2. Allow for open discussion. This question calls for opinion.
3. Allow for opinion. This is a conundrum of aesthetics.
4. We think much of the politically correct movement has come to roost on the humanities because the discipline is not rooted in the bedrock empiricism of a hard science but requires the exercise of abstractly held personal opinion. See if your students agree.
5. Allow for opinion. To our mind, the best one could hope from such a movement is greater tolerance of cultural, ethnic, and lifestyle diversity. The worst possible harm could be a trammelling of free speech and a kind of robotic censorship of the free and open exchange of ideas—the very pillar of the university community.

Rosa Ehrenreich *What Campus Radicals?* (pp. 49-55)

Answers to Questions About the Facts

1. See paragraph 1. The survey of college administrators revealed that at only five percent of all colleges did teachers complain of "pressure from students and fellow professors to alter the political and cultural content of their courses."
2. See paragraph 2 and others. She blames conservatives such as George Bush, George Will, and Dinesh D'Souza for stirring up the controversy for their own selfish political purposes.
3. See paragraph 10. Nervous.
4. See paragraph 9. The author says that two-thirds of Harvard students polled supported the war.
5. See paragraph 25. Because they would not only fear for their grade, but being "pilloried in the national press."

Answers to Questions About the Strategies

1. The thesis of this article is stated in the final sentence of the second paragraph, which reads: "To be a liberal arts student with prog-

ressive politics today is at once to be at the center of a raging national debate and to be completely on the sidelines, watching others far from campus describe you and use you to their own ends."

2. In rebutting the charge that left-wing fascism is taking over the universities, the author mainly focuses her attention on conditions at Harvard because that institution is one of the most preeminent in the country and that is where she attended school. Doing so enables her to draw on her own firsthand student experience and to marshal a host of specific facts and details to answer the vague charges of those who maintain that radicals are taking over college campuses. Her tactic is effective and works, as for example in paragraph 7 where she points out the chronic weakness of left-wing movements at Harvard, which is a representative institution.

3. The most serious weakness, in our view, is also the article's greatest strength: namely, the writer focuses too closely on Harvard as an example, when what critics are charging is a national, not merely a Harvard, conspiracy of leftwingers. Although the specific details based on her personal experiences at Harvard are engaging and powerful, they also limit her rebuttal to a single campus.

4. By admitting as she does in paragraph 12 that some left-wingers are a bit intolerant and could lighten up a bit, the author adds to her credibility and lessens the risk of seeming to be a rank and unrepentant apologist for the left wing. Her appearance of truthfulness is actually increased rather than diminished by this frank admission.

5. There are many instances of the author's use of irony and sarcasm to rebut the myth of political correctness, but our two favorites occur in paragraphs 20 and 24. In paragraph 20 she skewers Caleb Nelson by writing, ". . . In Caleb Nelson, Harvard has let us all down by producing a student so poorly educated that he's unable even to read the course catalogue"; in paragraph 24 she characterizes all the lurid public displays of yellow ribbons during the Gulf War as "Patriotically correct."

Answers to Questions About the Issues

1. Allow for open discussion. We favor the Ehrenreich essay since it seems to us to have a more reasonable and moderate tone and to confine itself to a less strident and sweeping line of argument.

2. Clearly we can infer that Ehrenreich is left-leaning in her political thinking based on her clear opposition to the Gulf War, which was an enormously popular conflict, and her stand on abortion implied by her criticism of Bush's ban on mentioning the term at federally

funded clinics. That she is left-leaning, however, should come as no surprise, since a conservative would hardly argue the idea that political correctness is a neoconservative myth. Note that she implies in paragraph 2 that she is a "progressive" in politics, which is a code word for "liberal" or left-winger. As to whether or not this knowledge should affect a reader's response to her argument, allow for open discussion. It didn't ours.

3. She is implicitly accusing him of sensationalizing the impact and scope of the political correctness movement. Sensationalism is a common charge frequently leveled against the press. Ask your students if they think the Taylor account is sensationalized.

4. Conservatives, one of whose central tenets is conservation and preservation of the status quo, fear that multiculturalism, which places equal stress on all cultures rather than emphasis on any particular one, detracts from an appreciation of western culture and the system of democracy that it has bequeathed the world. Whether or not this necessarily follows depend on whom you ask. Allow for open discussion of the second part of the question.

5. Allow for open discussion.

Chapter Two THE WRITER'S VOICE

F. L. Lucas *What Is Style?* (pp. 72-81)

Answers to Questions About the Facts

1. Answered in paragraph 1. By its association with a number of precious and superior people like Oscar Wilde.
2. Honesty and courtesy. From courtesy follow also clarity and brevity.
3. Variety, good humor, good sense, vitality, imagination.
4. Metaphor and simile. Lucas admires Americans for their native gift of imagery.
5. Mme. du Deffand: "You will be charming so long as you let yourself be natural, and remain without pretension and without artifice. Mme. de Charrière: "Have ideas that are clear, and expressions that are simple.

Answers to Questions About the Strategies

1. To"express" oneself is to communicate one's ideas; to "impress" oneself on others is to force one's attention on them so that they will be impressed. The first is good style, the second is bad style.

2. The image would no longer work because you would have a mixed metaphor. A person cannot drown in windy nonsense.
3. Numerous people could be suggested, such as Eleanor Roosevelt, George Bernard Shaw, and Beryl Markham.
4. These are the writers from whom Lucas learned how to write with good style. They all write with clarity and grace and were thus excellent models.
5. Paragraph 34 is a transition paragraph.

Answers to Questions About the Issues

1. This is partly mystifying. "Class" is used as a sort of rough-and-ready synonym for "style," yet it also has the nuance of gentility, refinement, or manners, but without the preciousness these words are likely to suggest. It is a peculiarly American idiom and used in no other variety of English that we know of. Allow for open discussion.
2. It does not, according to Lucas, since he adjudges some signatures as possessing mere flourishes and dangles while decreeing that a few others possess "style. " It seems that he is using an elitist definition of style to mean a distinctive and highly original flavor and definitely *not* to mean that merely being able to express a self confers automatically upon one a sense of style.
3. This is one of those "draw out the egalitarians" questions. Lucas means by style a personal and individual cachet that is highly distinctive and defining. That the individuals he cites as possessing this precious commodity are drawn mainly from elitist European salons is no accident; he is merely reflecting the tradition in which he was raised. Allow for open discussion.
4. Allow for open discussion. Lucas is mainly saying that style is the main. Of this famous adage Somerset Maugham wrote: "It is one of those aphorisms that say too much to mean a great deal. Where is the man in Goethe, in his birdlike lyrics or in his clumsy prose? And Hazlitt? But I suppose that if a man has a confused mind he will write in a confused way, if his temper is capricious, his prose will be fantastical, and if he has a quick, darting intelligence that is reminded by the matter in hand of a thousand things, he will, unless he has great self-control, load his pages with metaphor and simile."
5. Allow for open discussion.

Bartolomeo Vanzetti *Remarks on the Life of Sacco and on His Own Life and Execution* (pp. 83-84)

Answers to Questions About the Facts

1. Sacco is portrayed, somewhat romantically, as a skilled artisan, a family man who lives in a "neat little home at the verge of a wood, near a brook." He is also pictured as a man with deep political convictions. This somewhat idealized portrait reveals Vanzetti's affection for the man who was to die with him; it also says something about Vanzetti's generous opinion of his friend.
2. At babbling.
3. See paragraph 3. "I might have live out my life talking at street corners to scorning men. I might have die, unmarked, unknown, a failure."

Answers to Questions About the Strategies

1. The effect is striking and persuasive. The errors add a dramatic and sincere quality to the speech. This quality has been recognized and used by dramatists. In *The Male Animal* a play by James Thurber and Elliott Nugent, one character, a college professor, decides to read a portion of the Vanzetti speech to his English class to demonstrate that idiomatic English can be very effective, but he is opposed by the administration.
2. Plain, simple, and somewhat poetic. Vanzetti has a poetic feel for words; he gets away with using romanticized words like "heart" and "brook" ("Sacco is a heart . . ."). A native speaker would shy away from using "heart" this way; fortunately, Vanzetti doesn't. He has a knack for using simple and common words and spinning them into strong images: "a cursed past in which man was wolf to the man."
3. See answer to Strategies question 2. There is a lyrical and poetic quality about this speech that makes it worthy of inclusion in a poetry anthology. Vanzetti writes with a simple but starkly metaphoric style: "Sacco is a heart, a faith, a character, a man; a man lover of nature and of mankind. " That line is strongly poetic. His style sometimes rings with the simplicity of biblical writing: "He and I have never brought a morsel of bread to our mouths, from our childhood to today—which has not been gained by the sweat of our brows. Never."

Answers to Questions About the Issues

1. A philosophical anarchist is one who philosophically rejects the notion of government. The word "anarchy" has come to mean chaos and lawlessness; ideally, anarchy simply means the absence of government. The true anarchist does not believe that lack of government will result in chaos; his or her view of the world is more idealistic than that. The anarchist believes that government is a corruptive influence on people. On the political spectrum, the anarchist stands to the right of the conservative. This speech reveals nothing about Vanzetti's politics; however, it does show him to be a thoughtful and sensitive man. There are extremely lyrical passages in it. The broken language shows that English is a second language and not his native tongue. It was with speeches like this one that Vanzetti convinced many people that a terrible injustice was being done.
2. He means that their unjust execution will become a monument to the need for justice. In fact, Vanzetti was right. Many continue to think that Vanzetti and Sacco were executed for their political beliefs rather than because of evidence against them. A note in passing: while these men were awaiting execution, a member of a criminal gang in Boston was captured and confessed to taking part in the robbery and murder for which Sacco and Vanzetti were convicted. The confession was not allowed by the court, and in spite of numerous legal battles centering around the admissibility of the confession, Sacco and Vanzetti were executed.
3. None that we can honestly defend. Allow for open discussion. However, we can't help but believe that criminals should not be allowed to capitalize on the media limelight by writing memoirs or thinly veiled novels based on their crimes. The law that confiscates these profits and turns them over to victims is a good law.

Langston Hughes *Salvation* (pp. 85-87)

Answers to Questions About the Facts

1. Westley can be interpreted in a number of different ways. He is clearly not as sincere nor as intense as the narrator. He is already a little cynical as shown by what he whispers to the narrator: "God damn! I'm tired o'sitting here. Let's get up and be saved."
2. Answered in paragraph 11. He finally submits to avoid causing too much trouble.
3. The story is actually about deception. The aunt is finally deceived by the narrator into believing that he has accepted Jesus. But the

14

narrator was also deceived by the aunt into believing that he would actually see Jesus. Both the aunt and the narrator could also be said to be deceived by religion.

4. He has learned precisely the opposite of what the aunt intended him to: that there probably is no Jesus.
5. Hughes's attitude is probably best characterized as "sympathetic." He seems not to be especially bitter about the experience.

Answers to Questions About the Strategies

1. The narrative is framed to reflect the mind of a twelve-year-old boy in its use of short, simple sentences and a simple vocabulary.
2. A good example can be found in paragraph 4: "A great many old people came and knelt around us and prayed, old women with *jet-black* faces and *braided hair*, old men with *work-gnarled hands*." The italicized words show the use of specific details.
3. Hughes focuses on parts rather than on wholes in his descriptions. Rather than attempting to describe any one person as a whole, he focuses on the "braided hair" of the old women and the "work-gnarled hands" of the old men. His description of the church is synecdochical, as when he says "And the church sang a song about the lower lights are burning, some poor sinners to be saved. And the whole building rocked with prayer and song."

Answers to Questions About the Issues

1. Allow for open discussion. Some students will say that it does apply, others that it does not apply. Common sense tells us that people who live in misery are more likely to seek otherworldly consolation than those who live in lambs' wool. This, however, is often taken as an argument against the validity of otherworldly consolation, which it is not. The atheist in the bank is no more right than the atheist in the foxhole. Nor is the believer in his own bed any more right than the believer in the foxhole.
2. It is a known and documented fact that women are more drawn to religion than men. We do not know why, and we don't think anyone else knows for certain either. Explanations about the greater emotionalism of women and the greater independence of men have been suggested—much to the irritation of feminists—and much battered about on the cricket pitch of heredity versus environment. But there are no definitive and categorical answers as to why this difference between the sexes exist. Perhaps your students can suggest one.
3. Allow for open discussion. Social ostracism of some sort might well have been directed against him and his family.

4. Allow for open discussion. Many of our religious beliefs have rural roots, so it is not surprising that the "sheep, lamb, flock, shepherd" and so forth came into usage as staple metaphors. It is surprising that these fulsome terms have lingered to this day, when a wool sweater is the closest most people will ever get to a sheep.

Sullivan Ballou *Letter* (pp. 89-90)

Answers to Questions About the Facts

1. He writes, "The indications are strong that we shall move in a few days—perhaps tomorrow. " The occasion was a hint that his regiment had received its marching orders.
2. The love of country.
3. He feels a premonition that he will be spared on the battlefield, saying, "something whispers to me—perhaps it is the wafted prayer of my little Edgar, that I shall return to my loved ones unharmed."

Answers to Questions About the Strategies

1. The level of formality is rather high, considering that this letter was addressed to the writer's wife. Notice the expressions and phrases that we today would consider stilted—"Lest I should not be able to write you again. . . ," "that may fall under your eye when I shall be no more. . . . " This formality is partly due to the ancientness of the letter—people in Ballou's day expressed themselves in a way writers today would regard as wooden—but it is no doubt also due to Ballou's trepidations about the upcoming battle and his feeling that perhaps it may be his last, which may have led a poetic touch to his wording. Ask your students to compose equivalent sentences to the ones in Ballou's letter—as an exercise in how language changes.
2. The use of "shall," for example, which the writer engages in rather heavily, is nearly passe in much modern writing, especially the informal kind. Notice also that the writer uses virtually no contractions, writing "I have," for example, instead of the favored modern shorthand "I've." Notice also that the writer uses "thee" at one point, which a modern writer—except for those involved in the composition of formal liturgical prayer—would virtually never use.
3. The tone is elevated and solemn and is achieved mainly through the use of formal language mixed with poetic devices and phrasing. As an example of the poetic phrasing, point to phrases such as "to lay down all my joys in life"; "it seems to bind me with mighty

cables that nothing but Omnipotence could break"; "my love of Country comes over me like a strong wind and bears me unresistibly on with all these chains to the battle field"; "How gladly would I wash out with my tears every little spot upon your happiness. " To get an idea of how this letter sounds in the voice of a professional actor, you might try to obtain the *Civil War* video by Ken Burns and listen to its reading by Paul Roebling. It is wonderfully moving.

Answers to Questions About the Issues

1. We have heard it argued repeatedly that the golden age of literacy is gone and that no battlefield letter today sounds like this one, but personally we do not believe it. Many prosaic letters were written by Civil War soldiers, but like all things prosaic of that time, they have not survived and been preserved by the editorial scrutiny of posterity. We think this letter survived not because it is typical of what was written back then, but because it is truly exceptional.
2. We wonder about it, too, but obviously think the use legitimate or we wouldn't have included this letter in our book. Anyway, our reason for choosing this letter is not because it is private or intimate, but because it is lovely. Allow for open discussion.

Mark Twain *Advice to Youth* (pp. 91-93)

Answers to Questions About the Facts

1. Answered in paragraph 3. Hit the offender with a brick.
2. Answered in paragraph 5. He recommends being careful about lying or suffer the penalty of getting caught.
3. Answered in paragraph 5. "Truth is mighty and will prevail."
4. A youth armed with an old, supposedly unloaded musket that is aimed at a female relative.
5. Answered in paragraph 7. Good books.

Answers to Questions About the Strategies

1. The tone might be described as one of mock-moral earnestness, a parody of the kinds of appeals usually made in a homily. Its purpose is to set a stage of seriousness which is immediately punctured by the next sentence: "Always obey your parents, when they are present."

2. "Think what tedious years of study, thought, practice, experience, went to the equipment of that peerless old master who was able to impose upon the whole world the lofty and sounding maxim that 'truth is mighty and will prevail'—the most majestic compound fracture of fact which any of woman born has yet achieved."
3. "Always obey your parents, when they are present."
4. The ending is anticlimactic and surprising.
5. The word "bag" is a hunting term used to indicate a successful kill. Twain's use of it here is satirical and humorous, implying that the youth may be hunting his grandmother for a trophy.

Answers to Questions About the Issues

1. Allow for open discussion. The speech underscores Twain's view that people are essentially hypocrites, especially in failing to follow moralistic advice they so willingly dish out to the young.
2. Again, that humans are essentially hypocritical. Later in his life, Twain became cynical and confirmed in this bitter view. In this speech, however, although he carps humorously about the venal nature of humans, he does not seem rancorous or bitter.
3. Allow for open discussion. Traditionally, "character" referred to the moral essence of a person, the fiber and essential stuff which propelled one to make life choices between good and evil. Personality is the individual style of a person, the sum total of penchants, likes, dislikes, idiosyncrasies. Character, on the other hand, is generally thought to be a person's deeper and more essential nature.
4. One can find evidence throughout of a general cynicism and world-weariness about humans. Later, this attitude took a turn for the worse, and Twain became a full-fledged misanthrope.
5. Allow for open discussion. The point is that guns afford an often fatal amplification of human capriciousness, rage, and vindictiveness. They permit the husband who is temporarily vexed at his wife to translate and amplify this fleeting vexation into a spontaneous and deadly act. And vice versa, of course. Gun lobbies often try to peddle the equation of "us versus them," with the implication that if guns were only kept from criminals and the insane, they would be perfectly safe and respectable in the possession of the rest of us. Unhappily, humans are not so readily divisible, and gun murders and accidents are committed as often by "us" as by "them." Had the gun not been on the wall, the grandson would not have had the opportunity to terrorize the grandmother.

Ernest J. Gaines *The Sky is Gray* (pp. 95-119)

Answers to Questions About the Facts

1. He is in the army. We get the impression that a war is going on and the narrator's father was drafted, because Monsieur Bayonne complains about the father being taken and the family getting nothing in return.
2. He prays over it while pressing against the narrator's jaw with his thumb. He blames his initial failure on the narrator's saying Baptist prayers instead of Catholic.
3. See paragraphs 31 through 40. He remembers the time his mother beat him for his unwillingness to kill the redbirds he and his brother caught in a trap.
4. He vows that one day he will buy her a warm red coat.
5. She pretends to buy an axe handle.

Answers to Questions About the Strategies

1. The story is written in the first person perspective and shows us the world as seen through the eyes of an eight year old child. Other than colloquial or regional words or phrases, we would not expect an eight year old black child who comes from a poor and deprived educational background to use a fancy vocabulary. Point out to students the consistency and sameness of the narrative from start to finish, the way it holds to the viewpoint of its eight year old narrator without breaking the voice or otherwise wavering in tone and diction. This is not easy for a writer to do; it takes considerable skill and discipline.
2. It foreshadows the Civil Rights Revolution of the 1960s and early 1970s. Those who lived through this period will see in the young college student hints of the militant explosion in the black community that was to occur during the 1960s with the rise of such radical black leaders as H. Rap Brown, Bobby Steele, and Stokely Carmichael.
3. He does so through the use of language that is direct, colloquial, simple, and slangy. He uses mainly simple sentences and restricts his observations to the specific, tangible, and concrete facts and sights that might impress themselves upon the mind of a young child. For example, point out to the students the way the narrator discusses his mother in paragraph 4: "I look at my mama and I love my mama. She's wearing that black that black hat and she's looking sad. I love my mama and I want put my arm round her and tell her. But I'm not supposed to do that. She says that's weakness and

19

that's crybaby stuff, and she don't want no crybaby round her. She don't want you to be scared either." Notice the directness and the specificity of these observations. He does not guess about his mother's personality and he draws no abstract inferences about it. He merely asserts that this is the way she is.

4. The scene between the firebrand college student and the preacher in the dentist's office would have strained our credulity if it had occurred before we had become acquainted with the narrator's style and world view and had suspended disbelief in his character. What makes this scene tricky is that an eight year old child who is barely literate must recreate for us the ideas and language of a revolutionary college student without his account seeming implausible. The author pulls this off by delaying the scene until the narrative is well under way and we have come to suspend our disbelief in the truthfulness and realism of the narrator. He also merely reports what he heard and saw while professing ignorance about what it means. For example, in paragraph 96 he says about the college student's opinion, "The lady don't answer him. She just looks at him like she don't know what he's talking 'bout. I know I don't. "

5. The narrator keeps telling us that the sky and the river are gray, but it soon becomes clear that his entire life is gray, and that the grayness is an appropriate color and symbol for the harshness and deprivation of his childhood world.

Answers to Questions About the Issues

1. She is harsh because she realizes that his survival is at stake, that he cannot be soft and sentimental in his outlook if he is to live as a black man in the cruel milieu of Southern society.

2. This is one of the nagging questions about black families that keep recurring, and no one has a definite and absolute answer to it. Black families tend to be characteristically matriarchal with fewer positive role models for boys than white families. But as to the effect on the self-image of young black men, no one really knows. Some black educators, in fact, have been urging that successful black men take an active role in the primary schools to give young black boys a chance to see what they might become. Allow for open discussion.

3. The point he was making is that the society is a lie, that its inventions, definitions, and truths are arbitrary, false, and coined by the white society for its own narrow advantages. Proof of his argument is that the principles of the Constitution, on which the entire society is based, do not apply to black society. Since it is all a monstrous

lie, that the wind is pink and grass is black is just as real and true as any other assertion about life.

4. Allow for open discussion.
5. Allow for open discussion. That is the whole point behind affirmative action, to redress the grievous imbalances in opportunity that have shackled black children

Dorothy Parker *A Certain Lady* (pp. 120-21)

Answers to Questions About the Facts

1. Apparently he is her lover (we assume that it is a "he" although we have no pronoun to verify his sex) and he is also openly unfaithful and even confides to her about his dalliances.
2. She pretends not to care about her lover's romantic affairs, but is really hurt deeply by them.

Answers to Questions About the Strategies

1. The tone of this poem, in fact, utterly determines its meaning. Were it not for the tone we would not know that the speaker is plotting unspecified revenge against her lover—what kind of revenge, we can only guess. The last sentences, "And what goes on, my love, while you're away,/You'll never know" hints not only at the turmoil and pain she suffers while her unfaithful lover is scampering over the landscape with other loves but also at some secret amours of her own. Notice also the brittle voice the speaker uses to describe how she "tilts" her head for her lover, "paints" her mouth "a fragrant red" and laughs and listens to his tales.
2. It reinforces the brittle affectedness of the speaker's comments and helps us understand that she is putting on an act for her lover's benefit. Read the poem to the students without the "oh" and see the difference.
3. We know mainly because of the tone that is caused by a combination of overstatement, imagery, and occasional directness. We can sense the irony, for example, in the overkill of lines and images such as "drink your rushing words with eager lips,/And paint my mouth for you a fragrant red," or "And you are pleased with me, and strive anew/To sing me sagas of your late delights." Notice also that the speaker tells us outright how she really feels in such lines as "And all the straining things within my heart/You'll never know," and "Nor can you see my staring eyes of nights."

Answers to Questions About the Issues

1. Allow for open discussion. You might raise the issue such as relationships were more prevalent during the 1960s and even early 1970s where the worst effects of promiscuity could be easily reversed by penicillin. With AIDS ravaging the landscape nowadays, however, things are not so simple. Ask your students whether the fear of deadly contagion has made them more cautious and circumspect in their sexual habits.
2. Allow for open discussion. Certainly she was hurt while he was away, but her angry tone also implies that she was possibly paying him back in kind with affairs of her own.

Barry Bearak *Waiting to Die at the AIDS Hotel* (123-32)

Answers to Questions About the Facts

1. Answered in paragraph 2. The residents at the AIDS hotel are those who suffer from AIDS. They author says that "Nearly all are drug addicts" who were once homeless.
2. See paragraphs 7 and 8. They treat the admissions form as if it were a sweepstakes prize because admittance to the hotel guarantees them a private room, however shabby, with a bed.
3. See paragraph 13. Intravenous drug use.
4. Answered in paragraph 20. They are told to get onto the roof of a next door apartment building, scale a fence, and from there are guided by a homeless man named "Dog" to the rooms of the prostitutes.
5. See paragraph 63. That they will die alone and begin rotting before anyone finds their bodies.

Answers to the Strategies

1. "Remnant" suggests a leftover scrap—a discarded part or remainder of the broken whole—and its use here is highly evocative, given that these poor people are at the end of shattered, drug-addicted lives. It is one example of the author's deft use of imagistic words throughout this story.
2. "Ennobled" is an ironic word to use in conjunction with something as elemental as a "private room." The author is very clever with his tonal suggestions throughout the writing, part of the reason why this story is so vivid and gripping.

3. There are numerous instances that can be mentioned, and we will list a few of our favorites. In paragraph 8, he writes: "They return once more, this time waving that precious sheet of paper like a sweepstakes winner." In Paragraph 16, one of our favorites: ". . . its pale brick front marred by haphazard scribbles of graffiti, like a page in a madman's diary." In paragraph 21: "Conscience is scabbed over by expediency." In paragraph 29: "Their cheeks have sunk into gullies." In paragraph 39: "At times, he felt as if he were one colossal germ, with the smell of his wastes on him like a layer of skin." And in paragraph 47: "The memories pulse through them like the tingling in the stump of an amputee." The use of these images is largely responsible for the graphic and moving quality of the descriptions.

4. He adds a physical description of his own combined with the use of their own words to characterize them, quoting them no matter what the grammatical lapse or fractured idiom. For example, he quotes Dana as saying, "I love my sons so much, but all I do about it is smoke this s---." He also quotes a resident as saying about the apartment in which a neighbor had died: "The smell was getting worser for six days." This technique is highly effective because it is so well and deftly done and results in sharply drawn vignettes of pathetic lives.

5. In paragraph 26 he quotes unnamed residents using the prevailing lingo of the hotel, for example, "deep fiend moves" and "getting over." His aim is to give us a glimpse into the talk and thinking of the hotel's residents and to indirectly characterize the merciless jungle ethic under which they daily live.

Answers to Questions About the Issues

1. Allow for open discussion. There is simply no clear-cut answer to this question.

2. This is one of the implicit subtexts percolating through the national debate about AIDS—whether society should be more compassionate towards the so-called "innocent victims" who get the disease unwittingly through a blood transfusion versus those whose contract it through lifestyle choices. You should get a wide range of passionate opinions on it. Oddly enough, there are plenty other diseases caused by lifestyle choices—lung cancer, for example—for which this question is never asked. Ask your students why.

3. Again, no answer, merely a moral conundrum that your students are welcome to puzzle about.

4. Allow for open discussion.

5. Most of them seem to come from a blue-collar, working-class background, the author mentioning that "a few were mechanics, one a carpenter, another a nanny." He also says that one man owned his own carpet cleaning business while another danced at a male-strip joint. The point we wish to emphasize here is that ignorance about AIDS and its means of transmission seems deeply implicated in the spread of the epidemic. Class factors in as a contributory element in the residents' lack of education about the disease.

Donna Ferentes *AIDS Is God's Punishment* (134-36)

Answers to Questions About the Facts

1. Answered in paragraph 1. She says that her brother has descended into the abyss of himself.
2. Answered in paragraph 2. She says that the homosexual community uses the AIDS victims by portraying men like her brother "as innocent victims of a haphazard virus rather than as parties responsible for risking and spreading this most virulent disease."
3. See paragraph 3. She says that the family must struggle "for the soul of one already totally weakened in spirit and morality," alleging that the homosexual community, on the other hand, sees the end as the final opportunity "to accept their son's and brother's homosexuality rather than help them confront it as an accomplice in their murder/suicide."
4. See paragraph 4. She accuses her brother of worshipping "a narcissistic god, a reflection of himself," claiming that his every "lover was a compounding of this alien god as self."
5. Answered in paragraph 5. The author says that her brother used emotional bribery to demand that his family accept that "homosexuality is as, or even more honest than heterosexuality, no different from marriage, etc."

Answers to Questions About the Strategies

1. The primary premise underlying the author's argument is that there is a God, and that He (or She) is a caring and loving God who takes active part in human welfare and who attempts to dispense and teach moral lessons through viral and bacterial agents. Ask your students whether they agree or disagree with the author on her premise. You might also ask them—as some have—whether the fact that AIDS is primarily a disease spread (initially, but no longer) by sexual contact between men means that God does not disapprove of lesbianism.

2. This opening anecdote not only sets that stage for the writing that follows, it also establishes that the author deeply loved her brother and attempted from his infancy to consecrate his life to God. This opening actually helps the writer's argument by softening her image and establishing that she loved her dying brother. Without it, the essay would seem strident and its writer fanatical and unsympathetic.
3. Comparison. She is comparing—finding mirror image likenesses—the disease of AIDS with what she calls its "moral approximations." Notice the verbs she uses through this comparison—"mirrors" and "reflect."
4. Repetition of key words. Notice the repetition of the verb "flee" and of "lost."
5. In paragraph 5 she uses an extended metaphor of warfare to explain her brother's withdrawal from, and hostility to, his family. This metaphor, introduced early in the paragraph as "a fugue-like guerrilla war" is nicely rounded of by the final three sentences: "We watched him become less and less human, more distant from us, and also from himself. What he has never realized is that the bunker in which he has lived and defended has had all of the guns trained upon himself. One gun went off. It was AIDS." The image is effective because it is sustained and an apt description of the walling off with hostility and anger that occurs when a person turns against his or her own family.

Answers to Questions About the Issues

1. Allow for open discussion.
2. Allow for discussion. The image that emerges is that of a deeply religious person who, given her beliefs, is concerned not only with the physical wellbeing of her brother but also with the salvation of his soul. Those who do share her basic outlook about God and the afterlife might find her insistence on her brother's deathbed repelling and cruel.
3. Allow for discussion.
4. Society, we think, is ambivalent about homosexuality partly because many see it as a perverse and willfully made lifestyle choice that defies conventional behavior rather than as a biological predisposition. If it were ever established beyond a doubt that homosexuality is caused by a gene and not merely by an individual choice, we think there would be an inevitable change of heart and softening of attitude towards homosexuals in place of the presence atmosphere of grudging toleration or outright meanness. This change, however, would not come overnight but emerge gradually. Allow for open discussion of the second part of the question.

25

5.   Basically, she is asking him to admit that his lifestyle was a sin that offended God and to repent of his homosexuality as being morally offensive to God. Her brother, on his deathbed, would naturally find it difficult to face and accept these conditions since it would mean not only a repudiation of the way he had lived, but also of his homosexual friends and lover. Allow for open discussion of the last question about whether or not the sister in unreasonable for making these demands on her dying brother.

Chapter Three PURPOSE AND THESIS

Harry Crosby and George Estey *The Controlling Concept* (pp. 146-48)

Answers to Questions About the Facts

1.   Answered in paragraph 1 and elsewhere. The authors use "generative statement" as a synonym for thesis.
2.   Answered in paragraph 1. To give unity and purpose to a written work.
3.   That England under a Whig government and the Protestant religion was the best of all possible worlds.
4.   Answered in paragraph 7. That the reader ought to be able to put in a single sentence the central message or thesis of a written work.
5.   Answered in paragraph 7. They underline not the most important passages, but passages they found personally interesting.

Answers to Question About the Strategies

1.   The thesis is to be found in paragraph 1. It is: "Each composition has at its core a generative sentence that is the broadest and most complex idea in the work. It is this sentence that gives unity and purpose to the total effort."
2.   They mainly use examples. These are to be found in virtually every paragraph after the first.
3.   This is, of course, an appeal to authority, otherwise known as testimonial evidence. By enlisting Adler on their side, the authors substantially buttress their own case.
4.   "Definitive" and "generative" sentence. Why did the authors not define them, you or some student might ask? In fact, they did earlier, but not in the excerpted passage we decided to use. This omission points up one of the perils of excerpting. See the first question asked under "The Issues."

1. A definitive sentence is one that comes to a dead stop. It defines further what has already been said or is otherwise self-contained. A generative sentence, on the other hand, generates further ideas and sentences in its support. "Hamburger is now $2.15 per pound" is a definitive sentence. "Hamburgers are bad for your health." is a generative sentence. The first is a dead-end; the second prompts one to ask, "How are hamburgers bad for your health?"

2. Of course, the English mean that American colloquialisms and idioms are changing the language for the worse by muddying up its purity. We have no sympathy for this point of view, though it has aroused fervor in many an Anglophile heart. American English is brisker and brighter and far livelier than the stultifying, deadwood tongue spoken by the English. (There's nothing wrong with using "hopefully" as a sentence modifier, for example.) Allow for open discussion of this question by your students. Battles are still raging over some key words that are undergoing wrenching change in the public tongue. Among them are the following notable cases: "uninterested" is transmuting into a synonym for "disinterested," "infer" is being used interchangeably with "imply," and "snuck" is fast becoming the acceptable past tense for "sneak. " We don't mean to infer that we are entirely disinterested in this business, now that some suspicious coinages have snuck into the language through the back door of the vulgate; but when you think of it, what can one imply from this transformation but that language constantly changes?

3. Allow for open discussion.

4. Allow for open discussion.

T. H. Huxley The Method of Scientific Investigation (pp. 150-52)

Answers to Questions About the Facts

1. Answered in paragraph 2. Deduction and induction.
2. Answered in paragraph 5. *Experimental verification* refers to the process of testing and retesting the truth of a hypothesis.
3. Answered in paragraph 6. Gravitation.
4. Answered in paragraph 5. The syllogism.
5. Answered in paragraph 6. The universal experience of mankind and the possibility of constant verification.

Answers to Questions About the Strategies

1. He addresses the reader as "you," draws familiar analogies that everyone can understand (e.g., the example of buying apples from a fruiterer's shop), writes in short sentences, and use a simple conversational diction with no jargon whatsoever.
2. The thesis is the first sentence: "The method of scientific investigation is nothing but the expression of the necessary mode of working of the human mind." The chief advantage of making the thesis the first sentence is enhanced focus.
3. To demonstrate that it is possible for someone to do something all his or her life without knowing it by a formal name.
4. Immediacy and familiarity. Many teachers sternly warn their students never to use *you* as a generalized pronoun in their essays. Huxley touts that rule here and with considerable skill, achieving for his effort a colloquial directness that makes his explanations easy to follow.

Answers to Questions About the Issues

1. A life lived entirely by induction would engulf one under an avalanche of constant newness. Every experience would have to be retested for a conclusion, regardless of whether or not one had encountered the experience before. Conversely, a life lived by deduction would soon result in stale and hidebound conclusions. Stagnation and decay would be the inevitable result as no new experience would ever be allowed to intrude upon the known truths.
2. The syllogism is correct, insofar as it goes, but its major premise is flawed. This is an example of the principal danger of an over-reliance on deductive logic. One may use correct reasoning processes to confirm one's prejudices and arrive at false conclusions.
3. Allow for open discussion. One cannot help but feel certain that such sexist references would discourage capable women from attempting science.
4. Allow for open discussion.
5. This rather clever idea was suggested by the Irish essayist Robert Lynd in his essay "Superstition." Here is his reasoning on that subject:

> Consider, for a moment, how the first superstition came into the world. Man found himself cast into a chaos of drifting phenomena

without the slightest notion of what they meant or whether they meant anything. He could not distinguish between things and their shadows. He was as ignorant as a child as to how children were born. He did not know what was happening to his friends when they died. He was frightened of many things, because some things hurt him, and he did not know which did and which did not. All that he knew was that queer things were constantly happening, but they happened, not according to any rule that he could see, but in a confused and terrifying jumble. One day, in the forest, however, he casually picked up a pin—or, let us say, a sharp pine-needle-and immediately afterwards he came on the most delightful bunch of bananas he had ever tasted. This did not at the moment strike him as being remarkable. But the next day he noticed the same sort of pine-needle Lying on the ground and picked it up. Immediately afterwards he discovered another bunch of bananas even more delightful than the first. His brain swam with the sense of discovery. He beat his forehead with his hands—hairy, prehensile hands—for the birth of something absolutely new in his mind was making his head ache. He muttered: "I pick up pine-needles and find sweet bananas! I pick up pine-needles and find sweet bananas!" It was some time before even this conveyed a clear message to a brain unaccustomed to act. But as he repeated the words in a sort of trance, the truth suddenly flashed upon him. When he uncovered his face he was looking ten years older, but he was wearing a smile that was almost human. He did not exactly say to himself, "I have found a pattern in the universe, " but he had made the first move towards the happiest of all Eurekas. He was never quite simian again. He was like a child who, after long contemplation of the stars in the night sky, that seem to lie about haphazard like fallen apples, suddenly picks out the certain pattern of a constellation. He, too, has seen a pattern: the stars are no longer an abracadabra to him, but reveal meaning to him in a speech that he continually learns to understand better. In the same way, primitive man in his superstitions was slowly learning to put two and two together. What matter if they often came to five? It is better to put two and two together wrong than to believe that they cannot be put together at all.

Flannery O'Connor A Good Man is Hard to Find (pp. 154-66)

Answers to Questions About the Facts

1.   She didn't want to go to Florida because she wanted to go to East

Tennessee and visit some of her old connections.
2. The grandmother told them about an old plantation with a secret panel, and the children shrieked to see it (paragraphs 45-55).
3. The grandmother upset the cat's box, and the cat jumped on the shoulders of Bailey, who was driving (paragraphs 63-64).
4. He had killed his father (paragraph 117).
5. He says he calls himself "The Misfit" because he can't make his wrongs fit his punishment (paragraph 129).

Answers to Questions About the Strategies

1. To foreshadow what is going to happen and to make it seem probable-otherwise the story would be burdened by an improbable plot. The author is also careful to obliquely mention atrocities that the Misfit has committed against other people. When the accident occurs and the Misfit arrives, we are shocked by what follows, but not surprised by its improbability.
2. It characterizes the children as being extremely spoiled. This, too, needs to be carefully established in advance, since the children's outburst causes John Bailey to change his mind about seeing the house.
3. She is preparing the reader for the slaughter to follow. She achieves this partly by establishing an appropriately somber mood through description.
4. She suddenly recognizes her responsibility for the Misfit; it is at this point that he kills her (paragraph 136).
5. It foreshadows what is to follow. The family members are taken away into the woods and shot. In a sense, they have been devoured by the woods.

Answers to Questions About the Issues

1. The question is whether the willingness and the will to commit coldblooded murder requires some preexisting condition such as mental derangement or incipient evil or whatever. It is as much philosophical as anything else, and proof that society hasn't yet been able to satisfactorily answer it can clearly be deduced from our vacillation over capital punishment. But if the capacity to commit murder automatically presumes a state of mental derangement (otherwise, why would one murder in cold blood?) that is not found in everyone and that therefore restricts free choice in the one who kills, then executing the murderer is a bad case of muddled thinking equivalent of killing a person who cannot help himself. On the other hand, if cold-blooded murder is simply the evil exercise

of free choice, one must ask why some choose evil more freely than others. The answer might be that some are predisposed to making evil, wicked choices, which would mean that evil is simply another name for derangement. Ask your students how many of them would be capable of doing what the Misfit and his dopish gang did. Most will recoil with horror at the suggestion that they could coldbloodedly gun down a whole family. Allow for open discussion.

2. This ought to get you on the capital punishment merry-go-round rather nicely. Allow for open discussion.

3. I've heard it said that the children are typical Southern children and quite run-of-the-mill and ordinary. But they may strike some Southerners as absolute horrors and brats. Students will have various opinions. Allow for open discussion.

4. Allow for open discussion. There are some hints that the Misfit might be regarded as Satan. He seems in willful and open revolt against God, a sort of fallen figure much like Beelzebub himself, and admits to having once been devout. He is also a patricide, talks cant about Jesus, and is utterly wicked. Depending on how one constructs the case, an argument could be mounted for this interpretation.

5. This is the crux of the story, and a good deal of interpretation has been written about it. But one thing seems arguable. The Misfit's evil springs from his isolation, his withdrawal and removal from the body of humanity. The brutal murders he commits is proof enough of that. Christianity, on the other hand, is based on commitment to the family of mankind—care about the suffering of the universal other-with the recognition that the bell tolls for me and thee and everyone else. It is founded on the hard-won knowledge that we all sail in the same ark. The Misfit cannot commit to good and God because he says he wasn't there when Jesus raised the dead, but if he had been there and seen for himself, he would be different than he is today. What he lacks is faith. The Grandmother glimpses his turmoil and confusion, and realizes in a split second that he shares this awful predicament of hunger for certainty and longing for belief and faith with her and everyone else. That is why she reaches out for him at that moment and recognizes their mutual kinship. In murdering her at that instant, the Misfit renounces contact with humanity and again sinks back into the slough of egocentrism and pathological selfishness in which he wallows. That is why for him, "It's no real pleasure in life," for he is perpetually imprisoned in the limited self where gratification can only be fleeting and momentary. The Grandmother, on the other hand, though she is dead, smiles up at the cloudless sky. Allow for open discussion.

Edna St. Vincent Millay Dirge Without Music (pp. 168-69)

Answers to Questions About the Facts

1. To the shutting away of loving hearts in the hard ground. She is opposed to death.
2. "A fragment of what you felt, of what you knew/A formula, a phrase remains-but the best is lost. "
3. To feed the roses.

Answers to Questions About the Strategies

1. A dirge is a funeral psalm and hymn. The tone of this poem is angry and defiant rather than merely mournful as most dirges are.
2. In religion and art the lily signifies purity; the laurel signifies achievement. The line means that all, the innocent as well as the achieving, end up in the same dark and indiscriminate dust.
3. She uses rhyme unobtrusively—it is muted throughout because most of the lines are enjambed rather than end-stopped, which would have made the presence of the rhyme more pronounced. We think that the function of the rhyme is not primarily aural but structural-to add order and organization to the poem. Point out to students, for example, that because of the enjambed lines in the first stanza, the rhymes between "ground" and "Crowned," and between "mind" and "resigned" are practically muted.
4. Half-rhymes—that is, words whose rhymes are imperfect and muted— occur between "dust" and "lost," and between "love" and "approve."
5. The dead are all admirable and praiseworthy souls—beautiful, intelligent, kind, wise, lovely, honest, tender, witty and brave. None is stupid, cantankerous, cowardly, dull, obtuse, rough, ugly, and dishonest, even though these kinds of people must also eventually wind up in the grave. Naturally, to intensify the tone of sorrow throughout the poem, the poet had to concentrate her catalogue on the best among us, rather than on the worst.

Answers to Questions About the Issues

1. That it is too secular in its sadness. That the soul of these people live on and does not perish in the grave with the mortal body.

2. Allow for open discussion. We are not resigned. In fact, you could say we are pissed.
3. Allow for open discussion. The attitude in this poem is defiance, which is a romantic rather than a realistic outlook. As to whether or not it is a healthy attitude, ask your students for their opinion.
4. Allow for open discussion.

Malcolm Cowley *The View from Eighty* (pp. 171-77)

Answers to Questions About the Facts

1. See paragraph 1. An identity crisis in having to face up to being old and wrinkled when he may not at all think of himself that way.
2. The main virtue of old age, says the author, is an obstinate refusal to succumb to it and the willingness, instead, to battle its ills and infirmities. Its main vices are avarice, untidiness, and vanity.
3. The Langley Collyer syndrome is the tendency of the old to accumulate the junk of their lives and become extremely untidy. The author speculates that the old are loath to discard the things that have once been important in their lives, partly because of lethargy and partly because they have a strong instinct to preserve. Allow open discussion of the third part of the question.
4. Because they have nothing to look forward to and therefore try to capture the glories of their youth.
5. The author says that the old revel in the pleasures of eating, of sunning themselves contentedly, of being removed from the fray of everyday life, and of sleep.

Answers to Questions About the Strategies

1. He uses testimony from the aged, ranging from Gide to the Catholic poet Paul Claudel. This testimony is doubly effective, not merely because it comes from famous people, but because it gives a melange of authority opinion that credibly backs what Cowley has to say about the condition of aging.
2. This rhetorical question is used as a transition from one paragraph to the next, from the discussion of Langley Collyer to a discussion of the syndrome named after him.
3. The fact is that avarice among the old is so well known that Cowley can dismiss it as common knowledge. He does so by writing: "How often we read of an old person found dead in a hovel, on a mattress partly stuffed with bankbooks and stock certificates!" The lesson here is that one does not need examples to support what is commonly known and accepted.

4. The extended analogy of a battle, with combatants scrounging and gouging, the exultant shouts of the victors and moans of the wounded. Allow for open discussion of its effectiveness. It is a rather apt and graphic analogy that works very well.

5. It seems to us that it is, since writing about one's own infirmities and decline can easily lead to a tone of querulousness and self-pity. Moreover, such a treatment would suffer from being too personalized. This way, Cowley can focus on aging itself rather than its effects on his own body. He can broaden his focus to include interesting testimony from others who have suffered the ills of old age.

Answers to Questions About the Issues

1. Have the students read their lists out loud so that the class can discuss them. Students seldom confront their old age in this way; yet the exercise is enlightening.

2. In exploring their own relatives, the authors of this book found that the major reason for extreme frugality was the old person's fear (often unfounded) that he or she may run out of money and thus become a burden to other members of the family, especially the children.

3. Allow for individual responses to this question. Most students have answered this question by saying that they fear total disability most, such as suffering a stroke. They also fear blindness and senility.

4. The poem is a call to enjoy the challenges posed by life even after the body has become aged. It tells us that old age is the natural heritage of youth and that, well lived, it lifts human beings above mere brutes.

5. Allow for individual creativity in answering this question. The answers proposed in class should create merriment but also serious contemplation.

Marya Mannes *Stay Young* (pp. 179-81)

Answers to Questions About the Facts

1. See paragraph. The author says that to advance with aging, a man or woman must go "towards death rather than away from it."

2. See paragraph 5. The author says that American women think of youth "only in terms of appearance," whereas American men think of it "only in terms of virility."

3.   See Paragraph 7. The author says that advertisers should be saying to women, "Be yourself," and "relax," but what they are actually saying is, "Be young," and "compete."
4.   See paragraph 9. She says that in villages of France and Italy she is often struck by the natural beauty of aging women.
5.   See paragraphs 10 and 11. The author thinks that their efforts have cost women their identities.

Answers to Questions About the Strategies

1.   The author's frank admission that opens the essay adds credibility to her subsequent opinions by establishing her credentials to speak on the subject—as one who is herself middle-aged and facing the very creeping forces of disintegration she blames women for trying to conceal. It is one thing to be in one's prime of youth and scoff at older women who try their hardest to forestall the effects of aging, and quite another to be in that same boat yourself.
2.   The evidence is not empirical or objective, but consists of the author's vivid descriptions of older women who spend gobs of time vainly trying to make themselves look young. This piece was originally published as a magazine column and was intended as a vehicle for personal opinion. Nevertheless, the opinions advanced by the writer would seem shallow and empty were it not for her vivid and gripping descriptive details that reinforce her assertions. Point out to students that this kind of specific detail, done vividly, can make a generalization seem solid and true.
3.   She is making an implicit contrast between American women and the women of France and Italy who cannot afford the creams, lotions, and regimens necessary to hide their ages, and so allow themselves to sink gracefully and naturally into old age.
4.   She does so to personalize an argument that might otherwise seem too strident, vague, and remote. Her mother, in this essay, becomes the exemplar of what the author is urging women to do, namely, age gracefully and naturally.
5.   The final sentence of the essay, "Or so I keep telling myself," implies that the author is not as sure about her stand as she sounds and characterizes her as being just as vulnerable to the unrelenting pressures of the American tyranny of youth as those women she has been scolding. It is a touching and fitting note on which to end.

Answers to Questions About the Issues

1.   She means, simply, that we should accept death as a natural and inevitable terminus of life and not try to deceive ourselves into

thinking that the effects of decay and disintegration can be avoided. There's something stoical and dignified in this approach.

2. It should eventually make a difference when women are no longer viewed merely as sex objects but as doers much as men are, but so far we think the effects of feminism, if any, are muted. As your students what they think.

3. The author implies that advertisers are a primary cause of this tyranny, with their emphasis on using young, hard bodies to hawk and peddle a variety of goods and services; she also implies that overly abundant leisure time—note the reference in paragraph 6 to the "older woman, past her middle fifties, often alone, often idle"—and superfluous wealth are prime culprits—note that the European women are said to not have "yet found the means to hide" the effects of aging. Clearly women of Third World countries who do not have the financial means or the time to resort to the deceits of the beauty parlor industry have no alternative but to age gracefully.

4. Allow for open discussion. Certainly, there must be strong pressure on youth to conform to the prevailing ideal of youthfulness. And even the young are not exempt from pressures to always stay and look young, since they are also aging and there is always someone younger and pinker around the next corner.

5. It does not necessarily follow, but it is highly probable that any elderly relative who is striving to avoid her age is too mesmerized with the self to be of much comfort to the troubled young. Acceptance of self is necessary for wisdom, and those who fight the futile battle to deceive others about their age are unlikely to be wise enough to offer any sage counsel. Allow for other opinion.

Chapter Four PLANNING AND ORGANIZING

Samuel H. Scudder *Take This Fish and Look at It* (pp. 193-96)

Answers to Questions About the Facts

1. See paragraph 4. A haemulon.
2. See paragraph 10. A pencil.
3. See paragraph 21. That the fish had symmetrical sides with paired organs.
4. See paragraph 25. To look intently.
5. See paragraph 31. "Facts are stupid things until brought into connection with some general law."

Answers to Questions About the Strategies

1. The writer assumes a well-educated audience with an extensive vocabulary.
2. The essay follows a time sequence and gradually leads up to a climax—the lesson learned.
3. The humor is achieved partly through irony, as in calling a stinking, slimy fish by a fancy name like "haemulon." Some humor is achieved by bordering on caricature, as when the author emphasizes the awkwardness and clumsiness of the student. Humor is also achieved by reporting the students' sense of mischief, as when they made outlandish drawings on the blackboard.
4. Examine paragraph 7 for its descriptive details.

Answers to Questions About the Issues

1. Facts and their orderly arrangement are a necessary part of good expository writing.
2. The ability to see things that the unobservant person might easily overlook. For most people, a summer's evening is a summer's evening, but notice how it is transformed in the art of Faulkner:

   > It was a summer of wisteria. The twilight was full of it and the smell of his father's cigar as they sat on the front gallery after supper, while in the deep shaggy lawn below the veranda the fireflies blew and drifted in soft random.

3. Because drawing requires that one stare intensely at an object in an effort to capture its essential features on paper.
4. No doubt you will get many different specifics and particulars in the replies of students as they grapple with these questions. An apple falls off a tree—that is a fact. That the apple must fall because it is subject to gravity—that is a law. A fact is a specific and particular instance; a law is generalized principle that explains a category of instances.
5. Write about it. Writers often do not know how they feel about an issue or subject until they've had a chance to tackle it on paper. One is reminded of the remark attributed to Napoleon when a certain candidate was recommended for a job: "Has he written anything? Let me see his style. "

E. M. Forster *My Wood* (pp. 198-200)

Answers to Questions About the Facts

1. See paragraph 1. A public footpath.
2. Fcv See paragraph 2. It makes him feel heavy.
3. See paragraph 4. A bird.
4. See paragraph 5. It makes him feel he ought to do something with it.
5. See paragraph 7. Wall it in and fence others out.

Answers to Questions About the Strategies

1. Thesis: Property has four effects on a person.
    Introduction: What is the effect of property upon the character?
    I. Property makes me feel heavy.
      A. A man of weight failed to get into the Kingdom of Heaven.
      B. The Gospels couple stoutness and slowness.
      C. A fat bishop is the antithesis of the Son of Man.
    II. Property makes me feel it ought to be larger.
      A. *My* bird flew into Mrs. Henessy's property and became *her* bird.
      B. Ahab did not need that vineyard; he just wanted it.
      C. The more you have, the more you want.
        1. Happy Canute!
        2. Happier Alexander!
        3. Next the moon, Mars, Sirius, and finally universal dominion.
    III. Property makes its owner feel that he ought to do something to it.
      A. A restlessness comes over him.
      B. Property takes the place of genuine creativity.
      C. Creation, property, and enjoyment form a sinister trinity.
        1. They are often unattainable without a material basis.
        2. Property imposes itself as a substitute for all three.
      D. We don't know how to shun property.
        1. It is forced on us by our economic system.
        2. It is forced on us by a defect in the soul.
    IV. Property makes me selfish.
      A. No one else should eat my blckberries.
      B. The owner of a wood near Lyme Regis has built high stone walls to keep out the public.
    Conclusion: Perhaps I shall become stout, avaricious, pseudo

creative, and intensely selfish-until the bolshies come and take my property.

2. To sum up and underscore the theme of the paragraph. Repeating the topic sentence at the end of a paragraph is rather traditional, but it does add decided emphasis.
3. It is a transition paragraph.
4. Forster writes in an ironic tone and seems to be poking fun at himself as well as at conventional wisdom about property ownership. One detects the mocking tone in the apostrophe to Canute and Alexander, in such offhand statements as this one: ". . . so it is right that other people should participate in my shame, and should ask themselves, in accents that will vary in horror, this very important question.... "
5. The figure is called an apostrophe and is often used in burlesque writing or parody. Forster is saying that owning property gives one the appetite for more until one cannot be satisfied until one has reached the sea. Canute (995?-1035) was king of England, Norway, and Denmark. Alexander the Great (356-323 B.C.) was the King of Macedon and conqueror of most of Asia. Because Alexander conquered more of the world and therefore owned more property than Canute, Forster facetiously says Alexander was the happier of the two.

Answers to Questions About the Issues

1. That some things simply cannot be owned no matter how hard one might try to own them.
2. Allow for open discussion. There is Forster's essay.
3. Allow for open discussion. A popular answer will be that the individual acquires along with ownership a vested interest in the property and is thus likely to take better care of it. This is a rather commonsense notion but one that is demonstrably true.
4. Take one's life, for example. You cannot lose it unless you first had it. And once you have life, you are bound to eventually lose it. Something similar may be said about property: to possess it is to automatically and at some distant or near day lose it. There is a house in the Swiss Alps on which the sixteenth-century owner painted something to this effect: "This house is mine, but since I won't be here forever, it is not mine. Therefore, whom does this house belong to?" Dante must have had some similar sentiment in mind.
5. Allow for open discussion.

Alan Simpson from *The Marks of an Educated Man* (pp. 202-07)

Answers to Questions About the Facts

1. Simpson makes a distinction between liberal education, which nourishes the mind and spirit, and training, which is merely practical or professional or trivial.
2. The first skill is discussed in paragraph 5. It is the skill of thinking clearly. Among other things, this skill enables a person to see dishonesty and to be fortified against impostors of all kinds. Have your students draw attention to some of the shams in our society. Example: The argument that the poor can pull themselves up by their own bootstraps, but that they don't because they know that the welfare state will take care of them. This is a phony argument when we are faced with the fact that the majority of the poor are old, sick, or without skills to enable them to make a living.
3. Simpson moves to the second skill in paragraph 12. It is the art of self-expression in speech and on paper.
4. Simpson mentions three tests: sophistication, moral values, and the challenge of our day. The discussion in outline form:

Topic sentence: The standards that mark an educated man can be expressed in terms of three tests.

I. The first test is a matter of sophistication.
  A. obstacles to sophistication
    1. uncultivated home
    2. suburban conformity
    3. crass patriotism
    4. cramped dogma
  B. acquisition of sophistication
    1. in the classroom
    2. by mixing with people
II. The second test is a matter of moral values.
  A. blatant corruptions of our day
    1. horrors of modern war
    2. bestialities of modern political creeds
    3. vices of modern cities
    4. themes of modern novelists
  B. insidious corruptions of our day
    1. article in praise of cockfighting
    2. brutality for the sake of excitement

III. The third test is the unique challenge of our day.
   A. ingredients of the challenge
      1. acceleration of the rate of social change
      2. risk of catastrophic end
   B. requirements for dealing with the challenge
      1. versatility
      2. flexibility

5. The obstacles listed are:
   a. Verbosity-people's reluctance to use few words (paragraph 15).
   b. The decay of the practice of memorizing good prose and good poetry in grade school (paragraph 16). Have your students suggest a piece of prose and a poem that they think is worth memorizing.
   c. The monstrous proliferation of gobbledy-gook in government, business, and the professions (paragraph 17).
   d. Employment of objective tests in education (paragraph 18). Your students will enjoy discussing the pros and cons of objective tests. Give them free rein as practice in self-expression.
6. He holds up the humanists of the Renaissance as examples of educated men, because they wanted an educational system that would develop all sides of human nature: the body, the mind, and the character.

Answers to Questions About the Strategies

1. The contrast in paragraph 1 is drawn between a liberal education in the past and a liberal education today. In paragraph 7 the educated man, who has tried to develop a critical faculty for general use, is contrasted with the shrewd peasant and the illiterate businessman, who are restricted to their fields of expertise.
2. Coherence is achieved through parallelism and through repetition of a key word. In paragraph 9 the pronoun "that" is repeated; in paragraph 10 the phrase "There is the sham" is repeated.
3. Paragraph 4: Coherence is achieved by repeating the "little about everything" of the previous paragraph.
   Paragraph 9: Coherence is achieved by repeating the key word "sham."
   Paragraph 10: Coherence is achieved by repeating the key word "sham."
4. Various answers are possible. Allow for discussion.
5. The essay is divided into a discussion of the knowledge, skills, and standards that make up a liberal education. Throughout the work, the author repeatedly returns to this original intent in his transi-

tional phrases and statements. For example, in paragraph 2, he begins, "So far as knowledge is concerned, the record is ambiguous. " In paragraph 5, he again comes back to this threefold intent: "If there is some ambiguity about the knowledge an educated man should have, there is none at all about the skills. " And he opens the discussion of the standards a liberal education should offer with this lead-in: "The standards which mark an educated man can be expressed in terms of three tests."

Answers to Questions About the Issues

1. Various answers are possible. Among the liberal courses are philosophy, history, and literature. Training courses range from automotive repair and typing to bookkeeping.
2. This is a knotty one. Many English teachers will argue that standards are absolute and final and that there is no point in trying to compare Shakespeare with a potboiler writer such as Jacqueline Susann (*Valley of the Dolls* and other works of that ilk). However, it is not easy to explain this viewpoint to an audience who may not understand or appreciate Shakespeare while loving *Valley of the Dolls*. There is, admittedly, some element of relativity in the judgment of literary works, and it is hard to find and justify bedrock and unshakeable aesthetic criteria that will always show Shakespeare as better than a popular modern-day writer such as Stephen King. We tell our students that Shakespeare speaks the truth while potboiler writers generally do not, and since truth dominates the sphere in which we live, the writer who faces it squarely is better, in our judgment, than the one who ducks and dodges behind the uses and wiles of beguiling fiction. Allow for open discussion.
3. No right or wrong answers are possible. But it is an interesting point to bring up that perhaps one of the reasons why a liberal education is declining in fashion is because it presumes to impart ideas and attitudes that are not demotic. Countering this tendency of a liberal education to be snooty, however, is the existence of many diverging viewpoints and attitudes within it, some of which are open advocates for the common man.
4. Various answers are possible. Among the more explosive issues are nuclear war and the threat of it, worldwide hunger and famine, and the deterioration of the ecosystem of the earth.
5. About the only advantage we can think of is an administrative one. Objective tests are easier to grade than written tests and therefore may be administered to a larger number of people. The use of such tests—for example, in driver's license exams—provide a crude measure for filtering out the hopelessly incompetent.

James Thurber *The Catbird Seat* (pp. 209-16)

Answers to Questions About the Facts

1. See paragraph 4. Baseball radio commentary.
2. See paragraph 3. Special adviser to the president of the firm, Mr. Fitweiler.
3. See paragraph 6. Because he suspects that she is about to make changes in his beloved filing department.
4. See paragraph 14. That he is preparing a bomb to blow "the old goat higher than hell" and that he uses heroin.
5. See paragraph 17. She is not believed, is dismissed, and is referred to Mr. Fitweiler's psychiatrist.

Answers to Questions About the Strategies

1. Summary of story:
   a. Trial and verdict: Mr. Martin reviews how Mrs. Barrows invaded the firm of Fitweiler & Schlosser, and how her presence has been a growing irritation.
   b. Preparation for the crime: Mr. Martin follows his regular after-work routine; then, with a pack of Camel cigarettes in his pocket, he walks over to Mrs. Barrows's apartment. He plans to have Mrs. Barrows let him in, and then he will find a weapon with which to kill her. Once inside, he contemplates andirons, a poker, and a paper knife.
   c. Change of plan and perpetration of the crime: As Mr. Martin realizes what a strange portrait he is presenting, standing in the room with his gloves on, a new plan blossoms in his mind. He will drive Mrs. Barrows insane by playing the part of a madman. He smokes, drinks, insults his boss, and claims he takes heroin.
   d. Result of the crime: Mr. Martin's change in plan has worked. Mrs. Barrows is declared mentally ill and is fired. Life for Mr. Martin resumes as before.
2. The suspense is not killed because in the last minute Mr. Martin changes his plan.
3. The emotional climax takes place when the reader realizes that Mr. Martin is going to pull off an astounding trick.
4. Thurber prepares us by carefully foreshadowing the likely outcome. We are told that Mr. Fitweiler once said of Mr. Martin, "Man is fallible but Martin isn't. " We are also told in paragraph 7 of the late Mr. Schlosser's high opinion of Mr. Martin—"Our most effi-

cient worker neither drinks nor smokes. The results speak for themselves"—and reminded that Mr. Fitweiler sat by, nodding approval of this sentiment. When Mr. Fitweiler rejects Mrs. Barrows's charges out of hand, we are therefore not surprised. But without these careful preparations, the outcome would have struck us as improbable and stretched.

Answers to Questions About the Issues

1.

Mr. Martin	Mrs. Barrows
quiet, cool	loud, emotional
methodical	arbitrary
introverted	extroverted
dislikes change	wants change
operates secretly	operates publicly

2. Various answers are possible. The story is an excellent springboard to a discussion of moral values. Dr. Lawrence Kohlberg of Harvard University has proposed the following three stages of moral development:

STAGE ONE MORAL LEVEL

No differentiation is made between life itself and whatever physical or social value may be appended to life. Decisions are made in terms of physical or social punishment.

STAGE TWO MORAL LEVEL

The value of life is conceived in terms of a categorical or religious order of rights and duties. The moral decisions made are connected with serving the group, the state, or the church.

STAGE THREE MORAL LEVEL

Human life is conceived as representing a universal human value that supersedes other moral or legal values. Decisions are made in terms of personal, inner standards; the individual conscience is of ultimate importance.

Discuss Mr. Martin's actions in view of Kohlberg's scale.

3. Barrows is portrayed as the classic shrewish manipulative woman who uses sexuality and brassy tactics to overwhelm the good sense

of Mr. Fitweiler. The stereotype of the meddling and domineering shrew who refuses to mind her place has been with us for ages and has been used with vicious effect against women. Thurber's repeated use of this caricature has led some critics to label him a misogynist.

4. Allow for open discussion. Our views of the sexes, especially of women, have changed substantially since Thurber wrote this story, and it is interesting to speculate whether a writer today could pull this same story off. Certainly, modern magazine readers might gag on the caricature of Mrs. Barrows and find it offensive. Mr. Martin might be allowed to pass muster intact even today, but whether or not Mrs. Barrows would strike a modern readership as believable is doubtful.

5. Allow for open discussion. Probably not as well. There is a great deal of latent sexism in the stereotypes that make this story successful. Reverse the roles of the major players and the hypothetical Mr. Barrows will seem more quirky than funny. Miss Martin will seem a trifle unbelievable. Ask your students what they think.

William Shakespeare *That Time of Year* (pp. 218-19)

Answers to Questions About the Facts

1. The poet focuses on autumn, when the trees lose their foliage and the birds stop singing. The yellow leaves could represent people who are aging; the fallen leaves and the birds that have flown away could represent the speaker's acquaintances who have already died.

2. The poet focuses on a sunset, which again is like old age. The speaker's life is fading like the sun. Soon night will obliterate the sun, and death will obliterate the poet.

3. The poet focuses on a fire that is almost extinguished and barely glimmers. The log that causes the fire to burn is also the log that causes the fire to burn out. In like manner, the body that keeps the poet alive is also the body that causes him to wither in old age.

4. Paraphrase of the theme: When you consider how quickly life is over, you feel stronger than ever about all that you love, because you realize that soon you must leave.

Answers to Questions About the Strategies

1. Old age is like autumn; old age is like the sunset; old age is like a dying fire.

2. The poet moves from the general to the particular, from big to small: season, sunset, fire.
3. The succession of these one-syllable words with long vowels slows down the line to create a mood of gloom and sadness.
4. The rhythm of the line would be broken.
5. The antecedent is all of the images the poet has just described.

Answers to Questions About the Issues

1. That he is old and experiencing a fit of introspection about aging and death. In Shakespeare's day the average life expectancy was about thirty years. Under such circumstances, the question of death took on an especially urgent quality.
2. It is hardly likely that a young person in his or her prime can fully appreciate the wistfulness of this poem, and in that sense one may say that "youth is wasted on the young." Savoring this poem requires a creaky joint or two that come from middle age and the occasional fearful coronary thump in the night—none of which the young are afflicted with. Ask your class whether they think this poem a lot of falderal or whether it really stops them in their tracks. Most will say the former.
3. Allow for open discussion. We will leave the defense of this poem and others like it to the ingenuity of the teacher.
4. The fact that it bleakly states that the speaker's youth is gone and that old age and death are approaching while blankly offering no otherworldly consolations of any kind. Its tone is surprisingly modern in this respect and seems to anticipate the gloominess of existentialism.

Gore Vidal *Drugs* (pp. 221-23)

Answers to Questions About the Facts

1. He proposes that drugs be sold at cost and that each drug be labelled with its effect—good and bad—on the user.
2. A majority of high school graduates.
3. The lesson of prohibition, which was a dismal failure and led to a national crime wave and thousands of deaths from bad alcohol.
4. The Mafia and the Bureau of Narcotics.
5. He predicts that matters will only get worse. Most authorities and experts of addiction will agree that he has, in this instance, been truly prophetic.

Answers to Questions About the Strategies

1. Likely, the bluntness would be taken as arrogance. We are trying to point out here that Vidal is taking the liberties with his argument and topic afforded him as a literary man of some standing. His opinion matters because it is *his* opinion, not because it is necessarily an astute or cleverly reasoned opinion. That is why he is able to bypass the usual nicety of argument and get straight down to the bone—because he is Gore Vidal. The whole essay, because of this, reads like expert testimony rather than like a reasoned argument. That he is able to write from this lofty pulpit is because of who he is, not what he says. Out of the pen of a student, this sort of bluntness might strike many teachers as being arrogant and unreasoned. That's rhetoric.

2. To enhance his standing and stature as a quasi-expert. He is not writing from a "cloistered virtue" but from a streetwise perspective, which makes us more likely to believe him. This is what some rhetoricians would call an "ethos" argument. We believe him because of who he is and because of his admitted experience with drugs.

3. "Groovie. " The idea of crack addicts sitting around mumbling "groovie" among themselves is ludicrous. That's a 1960s word and currently has a quaint and grandfatherly sound to it.

4. To raise the views of the opposition and answer them, a standard ploy of all arguers.

5. The use of journalistic paragraphs—that is, paragraphs that are short and to the point and that contain only assertions and little or no supporting details. Vidal was writing for the *New York Times* and therefore was free to use the journalistic paragraph-indeed, he was probably compelled to—but students are expected to support assertions, not merely make them from a pulpit.

Answers to Questions About the Issues

1. The effect is one pinpointed by Vidal—that people finally begin to disbelieve the government's every pronouncement about drugs, even when the government may be right. Vidal points out that this has happened among marijuana users, and he is quite right. Many people use marijuana recreationally and have for years without suffering any ostensibly bad effects, or at least effects that are any worse than those caused by habitual use of alcohol or tobacco.

2. Allow for open discussion. No one knows, that is the problem, and it is in the minds of many people a horrendous social experiment to find out the hard way if the results are unexpected or bad.

3. Allow for open discussion. We think the forbidding fruit cliche has a modicum of truth to it, but we also think the allure of the forbidden is overrated.
4. A can of worms. Allow for discussion.
5. As of 1991, the United States imprisons a larger percentage of its people than any other nation on the face of the earth, including such countries as Iraq, the Soviet Union, and South Africa, which would certainly seem to add a dollop of truth to Vidal's assertion. Allow for open discussion.

Morton M. Kondracke *Don't Legalize Drugs* (pp. 224-29)

Answers to Questions About the Facts

1. He says that advocates of legalization love to draw parallels between prohibition and the drug war.
2. In paragraph 4 he cites these differences between drugs and alcohol: alcohol has been a part of Western culture for thousands of years, while drugs have been the rage only since 1962; 85% of those who consume alcohol rarely become intoxicated while with drugs "intoxication is the whole idea"; alcohol is consistent chemically, while drugs vary widely in chemical consistency, ranging from marijuana to crack to "Ecstasy."
3. The author says in paragraph 8 that marijuana is as addictive as alcohol but for cocaine users the addiction rate is 70%, about as high as nicotine.
4. Answered in paragraph 13: ". . . young people, who are susceptible to the lure of quick thrills and are terribly adaptable to messages provided by adult society."
5. Answered in paragraph 15. Some legalization advocates suggest "merely decriminalizing marijuana and retaining sanctions against other drugs." Kondracke argues that doing so would have its greatest harmful effect on young people while doing nothing to reduce the influence of the drug cartels.

Answers to Questions About the Strategies

1. He does this in paragraph 2 as an argumentative ploy which acknowledges the arguments of the opposition while rebutting them. In successive paragraphs he shows that the benefits from legalization are far outweighed by the negatives. To concede that some benefits from legalization would accrue is merely an argumentative tactic that puts him in the position to demonstrate that, compared with the disadvantages, they would be minimal.

48

2. It is, in fact, utterly illogical and begs the question altogether. The author assumes that one might drink alcohol while regulating the degree of its intoxicating effect but that no such moderation is exercisable in the use of drugs—one is either off drugs completely or on them and zonked. That, of course, is nonsense, and many drug users—of marijuana for example—are capable of regulating the degree of effect the drug has by controlling the quantity of intake, quite like the alcohol drinker does.

3. The thesis of his entire argument is stated at the end of paragraph 3. It is this: "In lives, money, and human woe, the costs [of drug legalization] are so high, in fact, that society has no alternative but to conduct a real war on the drug trade, although perhaps a smarter one than is currently being waged." Notice the unconventional placement of this thesis statement—at the end of the third paragraph—rather than at the end of the opening paragraph, as students are expected to orthodoxly do in their own essays.

4. The author argued in paragraph 4 that alcohol and drugs were significantly different for reasons of cultural familiarity and degree of intoxication. He cannot then turn around and use statistics about alcohol consumption to deduce probable levels of addiction to drugs without exposing himself to the charge of inconsistency. We think it altogether too great a leap in deductive logic to infer conclusions about users' probable addiction to drugs from statistics about alcohol usage before and after prohibition. If the lessons of prohibition, which argue for the legalization of drugs, do not apply to the drug scene because alcohol is sufficiently different from drugs, then the negatives of alcohol addiction before and after prohibition can similarly be dismissed. The author cannot have it both ways.

5. Since the whole idea of drug legalization is as much a moral and political issue as it is a medical or scientific one, the first question a cautious reader needs to ask is where on the political spectrum a particular cited individual, agency, or institute falls. On such a morally explosive issue as legalization of drugs, conservative bodies and institutes tend to favor repression over social experimentation and will promulgate any statistics that seem to favor their particular values and political point of view. For example, what do we know about the Research Institute of North Carolina, whose study is cited in paragraph 10. If we accept their numbers with the same fervor as the author does, the argument in favor of legalization seems utterly lost and futile. Yet there have been other studies that have projected much more optimistic numbers and figures than are reported here. The author seems to be snowing his readers with a mass of grim, doomsday statistics, and given the fact that this article first appeared in the *New Republic*, we

would caution anyone to first investigate the source before giving credence to the numbers.

Answers to Questions About the Issues

1. For us, it is the argument implicating young people as those most likely to be in the vanguard of experimentation with drugs, should they be legalized. Allow your students to express their own opinions.
2. Allow for open discussion. If tobacco were not such a widely and historically used substance, and if its terrible mortality were as widely known, we have no doubt that some governments would make a strenuous effort to ban it.
3. Allow for open discussion. Vidal certainly seems willing to give people the freedom to engage in privately practiced vice so long as they do not affect or harm anyone else and are prepared to pay the personal price. Kondracke, on the other hand, seems more eager to control and curb people's predilections than to allow them to practice their preferences in freedom. The issue of freedom versus restraint is one that characterizes, if only partly, one difference between the liberal and the conservative temperament.
4. Allow for open discussion.
5. Allow for open discussion.

Chapter Five DEVELOPING PARAGRAPHS

Richard M. Weaver *The Function of the Paragraph* (pp. 239-40)

Answers to Questions About the Facts

1. The paragraph is an intermediary between the sentence and the section (essay) or chapter. As a division of intermediate size, the paragraph helps the reader to perceive the parts of the composition. It helps to clarify the relationship between the sentence and the total composition.
2. The word *paragraph* means "something written beside." In medieval manuscripts an actual mark was used to signify a turn in thought. In Greek the word *paragraphos* meant a line used to mark the change of persons in a dialogue.
3. Paragraphs are compositions in miniature in the sense that if they are properly developed, they will be self-contained and have a basic unity and coherence that make a point.

4. A new paragraph occurs only when a new train of thought is pursued.
5. The paragraph must fulfill the same requirements as an essay: The subject must be definite, and the development must follow some plan.

Answers to Questions About the Strategies

1. Weaver is meticulous about starting a new idea in each paragraph.
2. Coherence is achieved through the repetition of the pronoun they, which stands for the key word *paragraphs*.
3. The first sentence of the paragraph is the topic sentence.

Answers to Questions About the Issues

1. The journalistic paragraph is traditionally short to the point of evaporation, has little or no specific details, and functions almost like a separate sentence. It is primarily a device of layout rather than necessarily a vehicle signaling a new thought. This use is justified by the broad range of readers to which such publications cater, and by the conviction of editors that paragraphs chocked full of details and facts would tend to repel the commuter-reader who dips into a tabloid to divert his attention from the noise of the subway. Students often ask why they are not allowed to write paragraphs like those commonly used by the *New York Times* and similar publications. The answer is that student writing is intended to teach a different set of skills than those practiced by reporters.
2. Allow for open discussion. Certainly the use of transitions must rank high among the other complaints. Good fleet-footed transitions are difficult to come up with.
3. Allow for open discussion.

Edith Hamilton from *The Lessons of the Past* (pp. 241)

Answers to Questions About the Facts

1. The paragraph is convincing because the topic sentence, "Basic to all the Greek achievement was freedom," is supported by examples from history. Also, the quotations from Demosthenes and Socrates add authority.
2. They have a sense of self-esteem and a desire for independence that give them irresistible strength.

Answers to Questions About the Strategies

1. The topic sentence is the opening sentence: "Basic to all the Greek achievement was freedom. "
2. The great teacher alluded to is Socrates.

Answers to Questions About the Issues

1. Allow for open discussion.
2. Allow for open discussion. Possibly one reason is that free people think for themselves and therefore act with greater initiative than people who are yoked in bondage by a tyrant.

William Somerset Maugham *Pain* (pp. 242-43)

Answers to Questions About the Facts

1. Some think it must be justified because of their Christian point of view.
2. The author's view is that it is nothing more than a signal given by the nerves that the organism is in circumstances hurtful to it.
3. Poverty is another cause of pain.

Answers to Questions About the Strategies

1. The analogy that one might as well say that a danger signal elevates a train.
2. The example of the effect pain has on hospital patients.
3. The word *also*, in the sentence, "Poverty also is pain. "

Answers to Questions About the Issues

1. Some people claim that pain (and suffering) produces compassion and endurance. Maugham is rather bleak in his outlook about everything in life—his pictures always show him glaring dyspeptically at the camera—and most vehemently so whenever he sniffed an aroma of Christianity in a doctrine.
2. Pain is generally regarded as specific and can be pinpointed to some physical injury. Suffering, on the other hand, may include angst or ennui, which, while unpleasant, doesn't necessarily cause the neurons to throb.

3. Trains are not sentient and therefore cannot react to their signals. The fundamental falsehood of this analogy is that it likens the living to the dead.

Chief Joseph *I Am Tired of Fighting* (pp. 244)

Answers to Questions About the Facts

1. The freezing weather.
2. The young.

Answers to Questions About the Strategies

1. Of the sixteen sentences that make up this paragraph, seven of them end either with *dead* or *death*. The effect is one of somber emphasis.
2. The language is curiously formal as are many of the constructions such as "Maybe I shall find them among the dead. " The effect of this formal usage is to add dignity and weight to the speaker's words. Notice that the chief uses no contractions—he does not say, "I'm tired of fighting," for example—and both his diction and syntax are curiously formal and standard.
3. "It is the young men who say no and yes," meaning that only the young men are left to make decisions; "My heart is sad and sick," meaning "I feel sad and sick"; and "From where the sun stands I will fight no more," meaning "From now on I will fight no more."

Answers to Questions About the Issues

1. Plainly, the Indian is portrayed as shiftless, brutal, vicious, and barbaric. In fact, history tells us that it is the white settlers who sometimes fitted these descriptions in their treatment of the Indians. For example, scalping, thought of as an indigenous Indian practice, was originally introduced by white men to enable them to collect bounties for killing Indians. Allow for open discussion.
2. Allow for open discussion. If your students say "none," ask them this same question about the children of Nazis and the children of holocaust Jews.

W. T. Stace *Man Against Darkness* (pp. 245)

Answers to Questions About the Facts

1. The picture of a meaningless world and a meaningless human life.
2. They regard it just as what it is.
3. The ancient problem of evil presumes that everything, even evil, must subserve some rational purpose, an assumption that is not shared by modern philosophy.

Answers to Questions About the Strategies

1. He uses simple words—putting the views of modern philosophies in quite straightforward language. He also gives examples of what these modern philosophies believe. The second half of the paragraph gives an example of one of these beliefs by discussing the attitude of modern philosophies toward the ancient problem of evil.
2. It is written from the point of view of "the most characteristic philosophies of the modern period. " The author says hose point of view he is reflecting in the above statement.
3. Much class discussion is possible about this. We feel it is begging the question to dismiss evil by saying, in effect, that it does not exist. The modern philosophers say that there is no problem of evil because there is no evil. Christians, on the other hand, say there is a problem of evil because there is evil. Both are dogmatic statements of belief rather than attempts at rational argument.

Answers to Questions About the Issues

1. Allow for open discussion.
2. The ancient problem of evil, in variation, questions why evil exists in a world created by an omniscient being who is presumably good. It wonders what purpose or reason is behind evil, and tries to rationalize away evil by saying that though we cannot fathom how, evil is for the ultimate good.
3. Allow for open discussion. It is possible to argue that without evil we could not perceive good.

Mark Van Doren *What Is a Poet?* (pp. 246-47)

Answers to Questions About the Facts

1. We expect him to be pale, to have long, soft hair, tapering fingers, and to go about constantly with an air of abstraction on his face.
2. We expect him to be absent-minded, incompetent, gullible, self-sacrificing, and a lover of children and pets.
3. They are more sensitive than the rest of us and are victims to their feelings.

Answers to Questions About the Strategies

1. He is attempting to describe the *stereotype* of a poet.
2. They are both sentence fragments. Generally speaking, sentences tend to have closure and to suggest completeness. Fragments have the opposite effect—they suggest incompleteness and continuity. Both fragments, in this context, are more effective than complete sentences (such as, "He is a pale, lost man with long, soft hair" or "He has tapering fingers at the ends of furtively fluttering arms") would be, since they emphasize that the author is constructing a composite rather than describing a real person.
3. He catalogues the attributes of the poet in the long sentence that begins, "He cannot find his way in a city . . . "

Answers to Questions About the Issues

1. Most of your students, if they cleave to the stereotype, will automatically reply that the poet is likely to be more feminine than masculine. Once they've stepped into the trap, ask them why so many of the great poets have been men, not women. Then allow for open discussion.
2. Allow for open discussion.
3. Allow for open discussion.

Lewis Thomas, M.D. *On Disease* (pp. 248)

Answers to Questions About the Facts

1. We were reassured that the greatest precautions were being taken to protect life on earth from moon germs.
2. The idea that the germs are trying to devour and destroy us.

Answers to Questions About the Strategies

1.   He explains how the lunar voyagers were masked and kept behind plate glass, quarantined from contact with the earth until it was certain they weren't infected.
2.   It was written for an educated audience. Most of the author's essays were, in fact, originally published in the *New England Journal of Medicine,* for which he writes a column.

Answers to Questions About the Issues

1.   Allow for open discussion.
2.   Allow for open discussion. We'll bet that most of your students say cancer

Robert Frost *The Flood* (pp. 249-50)

Answers to Questions About the Facts

1.   *Blood* can be interpreted as standing for violence and war with their resultant bloodshed. Other implied elements associated with the blood of the poem are revenge, ferocity, and repressed hatred.
2.   Violence begets violence, as all of us know who have watched the escalation of various wars over the years. One act of violence demands a return act as revenge—and so the bloodbath widens until entire nations are immersed in it.
3.   Since a tidal wave is huge and terribly destructive, Frost is probably thinking of war on a huge, destructive scale—perhaps another world war or the final nuclear holocaust that may destroy our planet. The stained summits signify how serious the flood—that is, the violence—has been. It has reached the peaks of this civilization.

Answers to Questions About the Strategies

1.   The topic sentence is stated twice, in the first and last lines.
2.   The word *water* is used literally to mean a flood of water, whereas the word *blood* is used symbolically to stand for violence and all that violence comprises.

Answers to Questions About the Issues

1. Various answers are possible. Roughly, the poem is about our bad habit of warring with and slaughtering our fellow humans in the name of specious causes.
2. Remember that Reagan once christened the MX missile, each MIRVed with ten warheads and capable of annihilating an entire continent, "the peacekeeper." Frost may be referring here not only to guises such as this one where peace is masqueraded as war, but to the murder and mayhem during times of peace. An "implement of peace" such as a statuette of the peace dove can also be used as a weapon to bash in a skull. That sort of reading can also be applied to the line. The point is, as the poet declares at the end of the poem, "blood cannot be contained." It can be let loose even with a diaper pin.

Joseph W. Krutch *Our Values Hurt the Environment* (pp. 252-54)

Answers to Questions About the Facts

1. See if students pick up on the era in which the essay was written (before 1970) when the following magazines were popular among mothers: *Good Housekeeping, Ladies ' Home Journal, Better Homes and Gardens, Family Circle.*
2. To the prevailing values of a society that insists on gross consumption of energy and goods, and on junk-piling nondisposable materials.
3. In paragraph 5 the author offers the following four solutions: 1) reduce the population, 2) get along with less, 3) find some way of making products truly disposable, 4) develop a system of recycling the residue. The third solution seems the least likely, given our present law of physics that matter can neither be created nor destroyed.
4. Sound economics and sound ecology are two philosophies that are irreconcilable; we must choose between consuming more and more and keeping our environment healthy.
5. The good citizen of the future will be one who prefers quality goods over quantity and who buys goods that last so that they need not be thrown away.

Answers To Questions About the Strategies

1. Paragraph three clarifies whom the author addresses: "*No one* has really faced the fact. We are still determined to increase every day the gross national product. . . . " In other words, the essay addresses all who have ignored the fact that matter is indestructible, and who are determined to increase the gross national product and to junk-pile discarded goods. That means all of us.

2. The essay consists of three parts: 1) Paragraphs 1-3 introduce the problem; 2) Paragraphs 4-8 define and describe the "disposable society"; 3) Paragraphs 9-11 tell the reader what to do about the problem. The two headlines make the organization obvious and keep the reader on track.

3. The opening phrase of paragraph 4—"The diaper, to take again this humble example . . ." draws the connection between paragraph 3 and paragraph 4 by presenting a glaring example of what the author has said in paragraph 3.

4. The final sentence of the essay is the author's thesis. It is well placed because it demands action and is the idea the reader will walk away with.

5. He defines the term by using examples—diapers, cars, wax cartons, and aluminum cans. Have students state whether or not they understood the term as the author defined it

Answers to Questions About the Issues

1. Have students present their views for critical analysis by the class. It will be interesting to see just how committed students are.

2. Encourage students to come up with items. Possibilities are these: recycling plastic bottles and paper, switching from plastic to paper bags because paper is biodegradable, or riding a bicycle to work or to college. Students will surely come up with their own creative suggestions.

3. For a proposed compromise solution, see Lester Thurow's essay on pp. 256-59.

4. We suggest you try ranking the problems on the chalkboard. Consider the far-reaching effects of such evils as smog, pollutants, deforestation, and so forth.

5. Allow for open discussion on this point. You might consider such aspects as driving horse carriages, eating fresh produce that has not been sprayed with toxic insecticides, having no plastic goods, or living without the benefits of today's medical knowledge.

Lester C. Thurow *Economic Growth Requires Environmental Compromises* (pp. 256-59)

Answers to Questions About the Facts

1. Here is a possible rewording: "If something must be done, then let it be done quickly." Thurow's thesis is stated in paragraph 2 when he argues that advocates of economic growth should agree immediately to implement environmental standards while environmentalists should immediately find ways to determine whether a project meets environmental standards. The watchword here is "quickly."

2. Because the poor cannot afford the luxury of vacations on lakes, where they might worry about polluted water; nor can they spend time in the mountains or wilderness, advocating measures to protect these places of beauty. The poor worry about buying food and having a roof over their heads. They want to work in factories regardless of whether these workplaces cause pollution or not.

3. West Germany and Japan because they have integrated both the demand for high environmental standards and the demand for economic growth by speeding up the process of environmental impact studies on proposed businesses.

4. Society (presumably through taxes), not the company, must pay the cost of retrofitting a business to make it meet the appropriate environmental standards.

5. He suggests the possibility of setting up a system of cheap compulsory arbitration, of the kind used in labor relation disputes.

Answers to Questions About the Strategies

1. The thesis/proposition is stated in the second and third sentences of paragraph 2, which is really the opening paragraph since paragraph 1 is simply a quotation. This is a traditional place for a writer's main point. Most teachers would require students to formulate a thesis in one single sentence. Of course, in the case of Thurow's essay, this could be easily accomplished by combining the two sentences into one: "Advocates of economic growth should agree to implement strict environmental standards without delay, and environmentalists should agree to cheap, speedy ways of determining whether a project meets environmental standards once a project is already under way. " Perhaps the author chose to make two separate sentences in order to stress the fact that the two groups are different. Professional writers, like professional

59

musicians, can break standard rules while maintaining excellence. Beginning students must be more cautious.

2. He seems to be on the side of economic growth and indicates his bias from the start by making economic growth a matter of survival for the poor whereas he indicates that a clean environment is important mostly to those who have risen above the need merely to survive. Industrial growth is presented as a necessity, a clean environment as a luxury.

3. He keeps addressing the reader personally: "If you look at the countries. . ." (paragraph 5); "If you reflect upon this phenomenon. . ." (paragraph 6); "Now [you] suppose that a family. . ." (paragraph 7). Such personal addresses are designed to draw the reader into the argument.

4. The brief paragraphs, free of detailed development, make this essay ideal for publication in a magazine, read by busy people on the run, who do not have time to read a long and detailed argument.

5. This is certainly not a lexical definition, but rather a definition that suits the author's economic or political purpose, which is to convince the reader that environmentalism is no different from any other consumer demand. Active environmentalists would prefer to define environmentalism as "the regard for conserving the natural environment of the earth in order to preserve it for future generations.

Answers to Questions About the Issues

1. Allow for open discussion.
2. This is a polarizing topic, depending on where your population of students come from. Allow for open discussion.
3. Many people allege, especially in times of economic hardship, that efforts to preserve the environment retard economic growth and causes stagnation. No doubt there is a smidgen of truth in this view, especially in some few absurd cases of bureaucratic over-zealousness, but the truly long-range view could argue that if we don't clean up the mess, economic growth will be moot.
4. Allow for open discussion.
5. Allow for open discussion.

Chapter 6 REPORTING: Narration and Description

George Orwell *Shooting an Elephant* (pp. 307-14)

Answers to Questions About the Facts

1. See paragraph 1. The young Buddhist priests.
2. See paragraph 1. Someone would probably spit betel juice over her dress.
3. See paragraph 2. He thought the British Empire was a great deal better.
4. See paragraph 4. "A story always sounds clear enough at a distance, but the nearer you get to the scene of events the vaguer it becomes."
5. See paragraph 7. That he shall spend his life trying to impress the "natives."

Answers to Questions About the Strategies

1. He is being ironic.
2. The story is told from two points of view: the official point of view that the author represented as a policeman in Burma, and his own human point of view, reconstructed in retrospect. His use of Latin phrases inflects the tone of the story with his official point of view.
3. The telling of the story in two tenses allows the author to frame the narrative and parenthetically comment on the story as he tells it.
4. Because there are remarks he is parenthetically making as he tells the story.
5. He compares his shooting of the elephant with a theatrical performance. The analogy is appropriate since he admits that he was role-playing for the benefit of the crowd.

Answers to Questions About the Issues

1. Allow for open discussion. Generally, roles provide us with shortcuts for interacting with one another, so that a novel set of manners and ways of relating do not have to be invented every time we, say, go into a shop and make a purchase from a clerk. Roles are the shorthand of everyday affairs and relations.
2. Allow for open discussion. They suffocate the individual under rigid expectations and manners.

3. It is characterized by ambivalence. On the one hand, he thinks that the Empire is rotten to the core, but on the other hand, he muses that it is better than the younger empires that will replace it. He hates the Burmese but he feels sorry for those who are victimized by the empire he serves. Allow for open discussion.
4. Allow for open discussion. He might not have shot the elephant because he might not have felt so pressured to play the conventionalized figure of the sahib. Being alone put the burden of the sahib role squarely on his own shoulders and made him rigidly act it out.
5. Allow for open discussion. Peer pressure is what we have in mind, and this question can open the door to a discussion of that volatile topic.

Martine Lebret *A Self-reflective Essay* (281-84)

Answers to Questions About the Facts

1. See paragraph 1. Until she was 6 years old she thought she had blue eyes.
2. See paragraph 2. The author was French, like her foster family, but her father was Haitian.
3. See paragraph 5. She says she felt proud of the "Black is Beautiful" movement but didn't feel black enough to fit in. She threw away her hair straightener and grew an Afro.
4. See paragraph 7. A German professor who was Jewish and whose family had been exterminated during the Holocaust by the Nazis.
5. The myth that skin color doesn't matter and that she's as good and capable and attractive as the white siblings in her foster family.

Answers to Questions About the Strategies

1. It is an effective opening because she places her puzzlement over her race in the context of her child's mind and shares with us her feelings of confusion and longings to look like her siblings. To mix feeling with fact as this writer does is always more effective than to simply proclaim either fact or feeling directly.
2. For two reasons: in these racially sensitive times the word "Negro" in some quarters is not only regarded as obsolete but slightly patronizing; moreover, the author no doubt wanted to indicate to the reader that the word was her mother's—for that was the word used during those days.
3. In paragraph 2 the author writes: "She explained to me that although I was in essence French like herself, I was also part

"Negro," albeit a small part, she tried to reassure me." It is poignantly ironic to hear her black father described as "a small part" of her racial makeup. The racial message being unwittingly given the daughter is that her blackness is somehow less desirable—and therefore to be minimized—than her French heritage.

4. This narration derives its narrative drive from the theme of self-discovery and self-acceptance of her racial heritage that the author subtly explores. Notice that she uses a series of successively different words to describe herself racially, ranging from "tan" in the first paragraph, to "colored" and "Negro" in the second, the "Black" in the fifth. By the end of the essay the author has arrived at a recognition of her racial distinctness and an acknowledgment of the pressures she has felt over the years and the need she has to be assured that she is every bit as worthy as anyone else though she is different. The growth of the author's consciousness about her race, and her self-acceptance of it, is the theme of this narrative and what gives it its drive.

5. The change that has taken place is in the author's frank admissions of her confusion and needs caused by her race, of her desire to believe in the myth that skin color doesn't matter, and of her identification with others who look like her. In the beginning she thought she had blue eyes and worried that she was too tanned. By the end of the essay she has come to a kind of grudging self-acceptance of her racial heritage and a frank acknowledgement of her needs.

Answers to Questions About the Issues

1. Allow for open discussion. Point out to your students that there are associations of black social workers who adamantly refused to sanction the adoption of black children by white families for this very reason—that they believe such an upbringing confuses the child as to its identity.

2. Allow for open discussion. We think he probably advised her to accept herself as she was and stop trying to become what she was not.

3. Allow for open discussion.

4. We can infer that it was a large family—she mentions that her foster mother had three other daughters; that it was Catholic—she talks about trying hard to please the nuns and blacking out at the communion rail during mass; and that it was quite affluent—she says she was sent to boarding school, which is not cheap. We can also infer that it was a racially tolerant family from the fact that she was accepted and raised by it.

5. We would guess that it can also be explained by the shared inter-nationalism—the author sees herself as French and spent thirteen years in Europe where she says she perfected her French and learned two other languages. So she shares in common with the Salvadoreans not only a racial heritage, but the common bond of bilingualism and participation in a foreign culture.

Floyd Dell *We're Poor* (pp. 286-89)

Answers to Questions About the Facts

1. His first reaction was to feel sorry for the poor children. This reaction characterizes him as an innocent child.
2. Because she did not want him to be embarrassed by the skimpy contribution he was making.
3. He reacted with humor.
4. His ambition was to become a lawyer. He also entertained ideas of making public speeches before large crowds and perhaps becoming president.
5. A bag of popcorn and a lead pencil.

Answers to Questions About the Strategies

1. It is passive construction, usually frowned on as being unnecessarily distant and formal. In this case, however, its use subtly dramatizes the powerlessness of the child, who could not replace the worn shoes even if he had wanted to. Obviously, new shoes would have had to come from his parents. The passive construction is further justified in this instance by the action being more important than the actor. In other words, that his shoes were discovered to be worn is more significant than who made the discovery.
2. The clues are obvious: the bag of potatoes his mother gives him to carry to school, the fact that the family itself dined mainly on potato soup, and the fact that his father was at home during the day with nothing better to do than read Grant's *Memoirs*.
3. These paragraphs ignore the obvious lapse in time between the beginning of the fall term and the onset of the Christmas season. Obviously, nothing transpired during this period to warrant more than a scant mention of the passing time.
4. The paragraph is compressed and short for emphasis.
5. To dramatize the climactic effect the recognition of poverty had on him.

6. The author was trying to convey the thoughts of a child. Notice that after paragraph 21, the vocabulary gets a little harder, as though the sudden, terrifying recognition of his own poverty had shattered the innocence of the narrator and robbed him of his childish outlook.

Answers to Questions About the Issues

1. Social psychologists have been telling us for a long time that poverty and want can affect a child's self-image negatively. In the case of the narrator, once he discovers his poverty he becomes ashamed of the dreams of glory he once had—to be a lawyer, to give speeches in the square, to become president—and quickly renounces them. Why? Because he realizes that they are pipe dreams and unattainable and he feels ashamed of harboring them, as if he had forgotten himself and his place in the world. Allow for open discussion.
2. Allow for open discussion. They most likely felt ashamed that they were unable to give their son a real Christmas.
3. A few odd facts about him do emerge from the tale. First, although the family is in desperate straits, the father is shown in paragraph 2 sitting down and reading Grant's *Memoirs*. We gather from this that though down on his luck, he still sustained his interest in the outside world and in history. We also gather that he is a man of some learning—he is reading a serious book of memoirs rather than a catchpenny tale by some pap novelist. (Grant, by the way, suffered such terrible vicissitudes throughout his own life that his memoirs would surely be uplifting to anyone down on his luck.) The father is also shown as characteristically reacting to adversity with good humor and stoicism, as when he replies to his son's revelation that today is Christmas Eve by saying that he'll go downtown and see if that's true. In paragraph 2, the author also portrays his father as sitting down to the usual gruel of potato soup with the comment, "Ah! I see we have some nourishing potato soup today!"
4. Allow for open discussion.
5. Allow for open discussion. Some say that the commercials make the poor more keenly conscious of their deprivation and want.

Tillie Olsen *I Stand Here Ironing* (291-97)

Answers to Questions About the Facts

1. Answered in paragraph 8. She had to leave her with the "woman downstairs" while she went out to work.

2. See paragraph 8. He abandoned the family when Emily was still an infant, leaving a note behind saying that he "could no longer endure sharing all the want" with his family.
3. See paragraphs 15 and 16. She always tried to find excuses not to go, but she never protested directly or was rebellious as her other siblings were.
4. See paragraph 18. The gift of comedy.
5. See paragraphs 26 through 33. She was sent to a convalescent home for children because she was sickly. When she came back, we learn her in paragraph 34, she became stiff and uncomfortable at being physically loved.

Answers to Questions About the Strategies

1. One good dramatic reason for not too specifically identifying the person or the reason for the call is to allow the narrator to review the totality of Emily's life from birth to the present-day. (Note—the person had not visited, but called, as we learn in paragraph 50.) Had the person and the reason for her call been too specific—for example, a teacher complaining about a poor grade in a subject—there would be no necessity for such a thorough review. By deliberately leaving the person unknown and his or her mission ambiguous, the writer creates a dramatic necessity for the flashback review of her daughter's life because of the call. What we can infer about the caller is that he or she is involved with Emily's life and is having difficulty coping with her—possibly she is a teacher. We also gather that she is concerned with Emily and wishes to understand her so as to help her in some unspecified way.
2. We take the ironing to represent the overwhelming drudgery of the narrator's life and her inability—because of too many children, no money, and no husband—to help her daughter in any but the most practical way such as ironing her clothes. The iron could represent the harshness of the narrator's life and the life of her daughter—notice the final sentence, "Only help her to know—help make it so there is cause for her to know—that she is more than this dress on the ironing board, helpless before the iron." This wish we take to mean that the narrator hopes her daughter will not be so swamped and overwhelmed with scrimping for the sheer necessities of life as to be crushed under it by endless Sisyphusean drudgery symbolized by ironing.
3. She uses a *flashback* that is prompted by the queries of the of the unnamed visitor. This flashback is effectively handled, beginning with Emily's birth and cataloguing the years upon years of neglect which gradually served to harden the child's spirit and cause her to

withdraw from her mother's pathetic attempts at showing affection.

4. She does so by shifting the way Emily addresses her mother, which ranges from "Momma" in paragraph 15 when Emily was four years old and desperate for her mother's attention, to "Mommy" in paragraph 20 when Emily is a little older and getting used to being left alone though still hating it, to "Mother" in paragraph 25 when Emily is now old and inured enough to be walled off from her mother's futile attempts that come too late to comfort her.

5. In paragraph 15 through the use of indirect dialogue the author is attempting to compress or telescope the various excuses Emily gave for not attending school. The indirect dialogue implies that these were ongoing complaints and excuses rather than specific ones made on any particular occasion.

Answers to Questions About the Issues

1. At the opening of the story, we are not directly told the age of the narrator, but we learn in paragraph 9 that she was nineteen when she gave birth to Emily, who is herself identified in paragraph 3 as having "lived for nineteen years." The narrator is therefore 38. Emily is nineteen, exactly the age of the narrator when she had her first child, and that is the parallel the author means to draw between them. We see Emily for what she is—an effervescent child—and grasp what it must have meant to her mother to be having children at such a tender age.

2. We think she feels guilty at having not been able to love and cuddle her first born as she was able to do with the others, and overwhelmed at the missed opportunity to comfort and console her child who has now grown beyond the loving ministrations of a mother.

3. Allow for open discussion.

4. Allow for open discussion. We think there is tragically an excellent chance of that happening. And so does the narrator.

5. The first-born child is typically reared with a theoretical and bookish strictness, and this passage to us means that even when Emily cried to be fed and the mother was lactating to the point of being in pain, she still held off nursing and observed the recommended periodic feedings prescribed by the child care experts. This is one example of how strictly Emily was reared with a rigidity typically applied to first-borns. For example, in paragraph 24, the narrator reports that when Emily called out for her in her sleep she would say, "You're all right, darling, go to sleep, it's just a dream," and that "Twice, only twice, when I had to get up for

67

Susan anyhow, I went in to sit with her." Ironically, when the mother finally unbent and wanted to comfort Emily later in life, by then it was too late (see paragraph 25).

Robert Hayden *Those Winter Sundays* (pp. 299)

Answers to Questions About the Facts

1. He built a fire and polished his son's shoes, before waking up his son.
2. Indifferently.
3. His attitude is one of regret.

Answers to Questions About the Strategies

1. It is written in sonnet form.
2. "No one ever thanked him" is more universal and hints of the greater miseries and ingratitudes that his father might have suffered. Moreover, the poem is, even in its present state, perilously close to being sentimental. Had the poet written, "I never thanked him," that might have been enough to make the poem excessively sentimental.
3. A metaphor.
4. The poem is written in four sentences. The technique is known as enjambment.

Answers to Questions About the Issues

1. The speaker's father was probably some kind of manual laborer. We gather this from the lines, "then with cracked hands that ached / from labor in the weekday weather. . . ." We may infer from this that he worked outside even in the cold weather and with his hands.
2. Any sacrifice or service done for one's beloved qualifies as "love's offices." These offices can range from the sacrifice a parent makes for a child to the considerations of a lover for a beloved—cooking a favorite meal, wearing a favorite piece of clothing, giving up a personal desire so that one's wife or husband will be able to buy some little treasure from the family budget. Allow for open discussion.

Etty Hillesum *Letter from a Nazi Concentration Camp* (pp. 304-14)

Answers to Questions About the Facts

1. See paragraph 2. "And God made man after His likeness." Allow open discussion of the second half of the question.
2. See paragraph 6. He caused fifty more Jewish prisoners to be shipped on the train.
3. This question is profoundly unanswerable. Allow for open discussion. Some historians have opined that Jewish stoicism is part of the reason the Jews accepted their extermination so calmly. It is still a mystery, however.
4. See paragraph 34. The latest guards were battle-hardened and cruel, with remorseless faces. Before, the narrator says, the guards merely looked puzzled, while these latest ones were jeering. Allow open discussion of the second part of the question.
5. See paragraph 31. By being entertaining and amusing the commandant.
6. Allow for open discussion.

Answers to Questions About the Strategies

1. She switches to the present tense, adding a sense of immediacy to her story.
2. She was obviously trying to tell the story of what was happening inside the camp. The details are too vivid, too concrete, too specific for her purpose to be otherwise. In paragraph 3, she writes, "One always has the feeling here of being the ears and eyes of a piece of Jewish history. "
3. The answer to the first part of the question is that she used ellipses to indicate the presence of the unutterable more, a line of thought she was either too weary or too pressed to pursue. No definitive answer can be given to the second question. She could be referring to the destiny of the Jews or to any other mystical speculation about her race. Allow for open discussion.
4. The *Oberdienstleiter*, according to Nazi propaganda, was from an inferior race; yet, he ironically dwarfed the German commandant, making him appear slight and insignificant.

Answers to Questions About the Issues

1. The description is realistic. History records numerous incidents of

human beings facing death with a smile and even comforting those who would be bereaved. It seems that in moments of ultimate stress, a human being can tap forces residing deep within the human spirit.

2. While it may be more pleasant to forget tragic events, society will be destined to experience the same cruelties and persecutions if no record is kept. That is why Jews insist on remembering the Nazi holocaust of World War II and Armenians insist on remembering the Turkish massacre of 1916.

3. Doubtless she means that the story will point out that some Jews were hypocritical turncoats, willing to betray their race in order to gain rank, status, and power.

4. The answers to this question will vary, depending on the student's ethical and moral code.

5. The editors take the position that an objective reading of reputable historical documents supports the vivid truth of the Nazi attempt at Jewish genocide.

H. L. Mencken *The Libido for the Ugly* (pp. 316-19)

Answers to Questions About the Facts

1. Westmoreland county, Pennsylvania.
2. The manufacture of steel.
3. Mencken thinks that a "chalet to hug the hillsides . . . with a high pitched roof, to throw off the heavy Winter snows," would blend harmoniously with the surrounding terrain (paragraph 3). A good example, by the way, of criticism that also suggests remedies.
4. Paragraph 7 implies a correlation between ugliness and Christianity. Paragraph 8 reinforces this impression: "It is that of a Presbyterian grinning. " Paragraph 9 asserts that this ugliness comes from a desire to make the world intolerable, implying that it is an extension of the Puritan world view that sees heaven as the ultimate destination, and earth as a way station to be endured.
5. They are infinitely better, he says; except in the more putrid sections of England, nothing comparable is to be found in Europe (paragraph 6).

Answers to Questions About the Strategies

1. "But most of all I recall the general effect-of hideousness without a break. " This impression is stated near the beginning of the paragraph: "What I allude to is the unbroken and agonizing ugliness, the sheer revolting monstrousness, of every house in sight."

The impression is developed by examples throughout the remainder of the paragraph, then restated again at its end.

2. "They have taken as their model a brick set on end." The rest of the paragraph elaborates on this image.

3. The color. Again the effect of this paragraph comes from its focus and concentration.

4. *Unlovely* is more powerful than *ugly*. *Unlovely* implies not only ugliness, but an antipathy to loveliness. That is precisely what Mencken is saying: that the people who live in these towns are revolted by loveliness and unrelentingly hostile to its presence.'

5. The metaphor implies a very powerful comparison between peeling paint and dead, infected skin.

Answers to Questions About the Issues

1. Without environmental preservation groups, such as the Sierra Club, the Audubon Society, and certain legislative advocates, the financial greed of industrial corporations and real estate brokers would prevail, so that the beautiful areas of our country would soon disappear as industrial plants, vast building complexes, and oil derricks would begin to cover the earth.

2. Allow for individual opinions on this question. One might argue that pretentious ugliness is especially intolerable because it is an act of vain dishonesty, promising beauty but delivering the opposite.

3. Allow for individual taste in this matter. Highway 101 comes to mind—following the seacoast of California from south to north—including some marvelous stretches of rocky inlets, white beaches, and luxuriant green hills upon which some lovely homes have been built.

4. Critics (Henry James, for instance) who accuse Americans of bad taste blame this aesthetic impoverishment on the youth of our civilization, saying that in a sense we are still barbaric. Opposing such a view are those who insist that America houses some of the world's greatest art. As examples of places where great art can be seen they will cite the Metropolitan Museum in New York or the National Gallery in Washington, D.C. They will mention numerous splendid structures, such as the White House, some modern skyscrapers in a multitude of large cities, numerous manors tastefully decorated by wealthy Americans, and certain beautiful public buildings, such as the Trump Towers in New York or the Rodeo Collection in Beverly Hills. One might further argue that antique charm is not the only requirement for beauty.

5. Allow for imaginative descriptions in answer to this question.

E. B. White *Once More to the Lake* (pp. 321-26)

Answers to Questions About the Facts

1. He was 5 years old when he first went to the lake with his father, and 42 when he went with his son.
2. See paragraph 4. The illusion that time had not passed, and that he could simultaneously experience the lake from the vantage point of father as well as son.
3. See paragraph 7. The author writes that when he was a boy the dusty road consisted of three tracks, the middle one being made by the horse or animal that pulled the wagon. But in the company of his own son, he discovers that the road has become a two-track road, meaning that the horse has been replaced by an engine.
4. See paragraph 9. When the author was a boy, guests arrived via the train and were driven the rest of the way to the lake by a horse-drawn wagon. On this later visit, he noticed that guests arrived by car.
5. See paragraphs 12 and 13. The sight of his naked son, pulling on swimming trunks over his bare skinny body, to go swimming in the rain.

Answers to Questions About the Strategies

1. Comparison/contrast. The author implicitly contrasts the lake with the way it was when he was a boy and with the way it is now.
2. It is a personification of the road as if it could nose its way down to the lake on its own. This is rather an effective way of characterizing heedless development, by imputing nosiness and meddlesome curiosity to a road.
3. They appeal to practically all of them. He writes about the lake's being cool and motionless (touch and sight); about the scent of the bedroom and the wet woods (smell); about keeping close in the shadows of the pines (sight); and about not rubbing his paddle against the gunwale for fear of disturbing the stillness (hearing).
4. Through the use of a wealth of specific details. Any writer can learn from watching this master observer at work. He mentions the green of the boat, the broken ribs, the leavings and debris in its bottom, and catalogues them in great detail.
5. First, because it evokes a comparison between the boy excitedly wiggling into his wet trunks and wincing as they touch his vital parts and the author suddenly feeling the chill of his own mortality in the same place. Second, because it is the seat of life from which

the boy's own life sprung. The image of the chill of death felt in the groin thus nicely rounds off the sudden realization, denied until now, that the author is aging and soon must face his own demise.

Answers to Questions About the Issues

1. White labels the lake spot "holy" because in his mind it loomed as an ideal place, having left him with many memories of pleasurable beauty. The passage of time had, as it always does, erased all of the bad memories, leaving only the good. The poet Emily Dickinson once wrote that for each of us Eden is the past, remembered as idyllic and perfect. For White, time had elevated the lake to a sacred spot. Allow for varied answers to the last part of the question.

2. Allow the students to use their imaginations. Is it possible that most people could be using airborne vehicles of transportation-individual flying machines?

3. The implication is that some people were refined and therefore socially acceptable whereas others had poor manners and were therefore shunned. Times have not changed in this respect. Campers, especially, abide by certain rules of decorum: keeping the grounds clean, keeping the noise down at night, being helpful when needed, avoiding crude language in front of children, and so forth.

4. Many middle-aged people are thankful that they no longer feel compelled to be daring, adventuresome, or tireless. They would think of how pleasant it was not to slip into a cold, wet bathing suit in order to swim in the rain, but instead to read a good book in the warmth and coziness of a dry cabin.

5. Allow for individual examples. Most youths seem to consider themselves immortal-as indicated by their daredevil acts, such as surfing high waves, jumping wild rapids, exploring treacherous glaciers, climbing steep canyon walls, and driving at breakneck speeds. Nevertheless, if asked to think about the subject, even a college student will doubtless name some experience that taught him or her that human beings are all mortal. Allow for a variety of answers on the second question.

James Joyce *Hell* (pp. 328-30)

Answers to Questions About the Facts

1. Four thousand miles thick (paragraph 1).

2. It burns black, giving out no light; moreover, it burns but does not destroy (paragraphs 2, 4).
3. The fire (paragraph 4).
4. It comes directly from the anger of God (paragraph 6).
5. They were placed in a sack with a cock, a monkey, and a serpent, and cast into the sea (paragraph 7). 7).

Answers to Questions About the Strategies

1. The description systematically breaks down the torments of hell and treats each in separate paragraphs. Paragraph 1 treats the narrowness of hell; paragraph 2, its darkness; paragraph 3, its stench; paragraphs 4, 5, and 6, its fire; paragraph 7, the noises made by the damned.
2. This paragraph contrasts the fire of earth with the fire in hell. Its purpose is to evoke and use the listeners' familiarity with "earthly fire" in the description of hellfire. To a lesser extent, paragraph 5 continues this.
3. Again, to evoke and use the listeners' experience (familiarity with earthly prisons) in the description of something remote (the prison of hell). The Jesuit preacher-and research has indicated that Joyce based this description on a published sermon—needs to do this because he is attempting to describe a place that no one alive has ever seen or ever will see, and that no dead person has returned to describe accurately.
4. The paragraph begins with a generality and ends with a specific and detailed description of a burning sinner. Concrete detail is skillfully used in this paragraph and throughout the selection. It should be pointed out to the students that the key to effective writing is the enumeration of specific and concrete details: "The blood seethes and boils in the veins," and so on.
5. He addresses the description to the listeners, inviting their active participation. Frequently he exhorts them to "imagine" what he is describing, as in paragraph 3. In paragraph 4 he invites his listeners to place a finger in the flame of a candle and feel the pain of fire.

Answers to Questions About the Issues

1. Modern hell has been portrayed in various ways. For instance, the French existentialist Jean-Paul Sartre stated that "Hell is other people," stressing the misery human beings cause each other when they are incapable of love or compassion. Robert Frost wrote a poem indicating that fire is only one concept of how the world will end; another is ice. The idea behind the poem is that while fire

represents passionate anger and hatred, ice represents total indifference. Frost's ironic message is that total indifference is perhaps more devastating than passionate hatred. Allow students to imagine what for them might constitute the ultimate hell.

2. Depending on one's personal beliefs, the answers to the questions will be either religious or scientific. The religious person will doubtless claim that God has instilled in human beings a desire for immortality and that God intends to reward good lives with Paradise and evil lives with Hell. The scientific rationalist, on the other hand, may say that the propagation of the species depends on the ability to avoid death; in short, anything that promotes life ultimately is good, but anything that extinguishes life ultimately is evil. Consequently, people's fear of extinction has caused them to invent a paradise for the good and a hell for the evil. Some modernists, of course, believe in the cyclical renewal of life and are satisfied that death for the individual means biological disintegration with no extension of life into the hereafter except through progeny. Allow for varying opinions on the last half of the question.

3. Doubtless such a sermon will frighten youth into submission. Allow for varying views on whether or not fear is a good and effective way to teach human behavior.

4. Allow students to express their individual views on this question.

5. In the final paragraph. Both Dante and Joyce take the position that exerting an evil influence on another person is one of the worst sins.

Eudora Welty *A Worn Path* (pp. 332-39)

Answers to Questions About the Facts

1. The author compares Phoenix Jackson's walk to the moving pendulum in a grandfather clock. Because she is old and somewhat unstable on her feet, Phoenix keeps her balance by planting her steps wide apart. This movement from side to side is remindful of the back-and-forth movement of a clock pendulum. Later on, in paragraph 78, one of the nurses says, "She makes these trips just as regular as clockwork."

2. Phoenix Jackson is on her way to the hospital in order to replenish the medicine her little grandson must have because years earlier he had damaged his throat by swallowing some lye. The medicine will soothe the little boy's pain.

3. Crossing the creek by walking on a log. She keeps herself from falling by using her cane for balance.

4. She imagines that a little boy is offering her a slice of marble cake (paragraph 15); she mistakes a scarecrow for a man and talks to him (paragraphs 22-28); when the nurse first asks her about her grandson, she cannot remember why she is at the hospital (paragraphs 79-91).
5. She blames her loss of memory on the fact that when the South surrendered to the North at the end of the Civil War, she was too old to go to school and acquire an education (see paragraph 90).

Answers to Questions About the Strategies

1. The plot consists of tracing Phoenix Jackson's journey from home to the hospital. The conflict arises from Phoenix's fierce determination pitted against the obstacles on the journey. The conflict is resolved when Phoenix achieves her goal of getting the medicine for her grandchild.
2. Phoenix's speech tells us that she is a southern Negro, that she lacks formal education, and that she has a natural sense of poetry.
3. See paragraphs 16 through 28. The humor arises from Phoenix's superstitious nature. She is suspicious of buzzards, she believes in two-headed snakes, and she is afraid of ghosts. The humor comes close to caricature when Phoenix starts to dance with the scarecrow.
4. The story takes place some decades after the Civil War, because Phoenix was young when Lee surrendered at Appomattox.
5. She appears to be a knight in shining armor, resting after attempting a great feat such as slaying a dragon or making a religious crusade. Sitting there, Phoenix acquires heroic dimensions.

Answers to Questions About the Issues

1. Each year Phoenix Jackson makes an arduous journey to bring medicine to her grandson. She rises from the ashes of old age to perform this life giving act. Her burnished skin and her red scarf are suggestive of the plumage of the phoenix bird.
2. The dominant impression is dignified old age. Phoenix is old and poor, but she is neat and she moves purposefully.
3. Phoenix is old and somewhat senile. She talks out loud in order to encourage herself. Her expressions reflect the language of her locality.
4. Apparently Phoenix is used to grubbing for a living. She probably has subsisted on the leftovers of people who have more than she has. Also, she plans to use the money for her grandchild. She knows that God sees her deed, but she is not concerned. Perhaps

76

she knows He will understand. Have your students discuss the morality of Phoenix's deed.

5. The story is remindful of the journey of the Magi. Phoenix is bringing a gift for her grandchild. She is committed to her journey.

6. In mythological quests, a protagonist sets out on a journey to accomplish some heroic deed. In the process, he or she must overcome difficult obstacles. In a sense, Phoenix's journey represents the arduous history of blacks in the United States

May Swenson *Pigeon Woman* (pp. 341-42)

Answers to Questions About the Facts

1. The pigeon woman is an old, grotesquely gaudy woman. In terms of her looks, she could play the part of a witch in a fairy tale.

2. As we see her loneliness and how she substitutes the brief attention from the pigeons for human love, we feel compassion for her rather than derision.

3. The woman pretends that she is young and that to feed the pigeons is her job; so she is punctual and she dresses up, albeit in an eccentric way, for the pigeons.

4. The pigeons are opportunistic: they converge on the woman as long as she has food to give them, but when the crumbs are gone they leave her, lonely and unwanted.

5. Thousands of people like her exist all over the country-lost souls, unwanted, left to find companionship and meaning as best they can. Have your students suggest ways in which society can improve the lot of these socially alienated people.

Answers to Questions About the Strategies

1. Expressions such as "flat gym shoes," "blue knots," "she squats," and "to treat" have a mundane flavor. The use of "1:30" in numerals tends toward informality, as does the contraction "she'd" in line 13. The general informality of the language creates a contemporary atmosphere.

2. As the pigeons cluster together, hopping about, they look like a windswept, slate-gray lake into which the pigeon lady wades.

3. The pigeon woman has varicose veins. While this image is not romantic, it is visually concrete.

4. Feathers are decorative. The woman has dyed her hair a bright orange in order to attract the pigeons, as peacocks preen to attract a mate.

5. Flint is a hard, quartzlike substance. When the pigeons withdraw, they exemplify the hard cruelty of a person who withdraws his love from one who desires it.

Answers to Questions About the Issues

1. Encourage some creative suggestions. For instance, some cities have opened temporary camping grounds, established missions that provide free nourishment, or placed some of the more helpless women in halfway houses, where certain families receive money from the government in exchange for supplying these victims with room and board. In his September 1987 visit to the United States, Pope John Paul II urged the United States to do everything in its power to help care for the hungry, the poor, and the helpless in our country.
2. The woman feels needed by the pigeons. Most psychiatrists indicate that people lose hope when they are no longer needed or when they believe that no one cares. Loss of hope can lead to despair, and despair to a desire for death.
3. She could adopt a stray cat or dog. Pets have been known to save many elderly people from ultimate loneliness. Allow for other creative suggestions.
4. Allow for individual descriptions.
5. The following suggestions have been proposed:
   a. Strengthen the expanded family by encouraging its successful members to take responsibility for those in the family who cannot properly care for themselves.
   b. Build and maintain clean, pleasant government institutions to care for the helplessly poor.
   c. Require retirement plans for all citizens so that they can properly provide for themselves in old age.
   d. Establish more free health clinics, where the poor and debilitated can receive help in highly populated areas.
   Other poems about lonely old people: Wordsworth's "Resolution and Independence" and Frost's "An Old Man's Winter Night."

Will Durant *The Spartan Code* (pp. 346-50)

Answers to Questions About the Facts

1. Answered in the first paragraph. Eugenics, says the author, was the first step in producing the Spartan man. If a child was judged defective upon birth by a state council of inspectors, the infant was thrown from Mt. Taygetus to its death on the rocks below.

78

2. See paragraph 2. He was taken from his parents' home and reared in a state military school where he was taught military discipline combined with scholastics.

3. See paragraphs 4 and 5. They were raised at home but were made to participate in vigorous games such as running and wrestling to condition them for motherhood. The author says that mental training was not wasted on Spartan girls.

4. See paragraphs 6. They were excluded from the right to vote, were banned from public processions, and were often roughed up by women in the streets. The author says that in Sparta it was a crime to be celibate.

5. See paragraph 8. They enjoyed a position in society, says the author, and were considerably better than women elsewhere in Greece, with the right to inherit wealth and bequeath property. The author writes: "They lived a life of luxury and liberty at home while the men bore the brunt of frequent war, or dined on simple fare in the public mess."

Answers to Questions About the Strategies

1. He uses a roughly chronological organization, beginning with the practice of eugenics before birth, the custom of infanticide after birth, and then the rearing of the sons that takes place between the ages of seven through thirty. After discussing the customs of the state mandated training for boys, he segues to the training of girls, to the customs of mating and marriage mandated by the state, and then to the status of women in Sparta. His final section deals with the treatment of adult men in Sparta and the relationship of the state to foreigners.

2. Up to paragraph 8, the discussion has described the sequence of training to which a Sparta boy was subjected followed by briefer coverage of the training of Spartan women. Paragraph 9 then launches into the treatment of adult Spartan men, while paragraphs 10 and 11 give an overview of Spartan customs and how the state was viewed by, and itself viewed, foreigners. This is a sufficiently major change of topic to justify the use of a section break.

3. We think the immense popularity of Durant's histories can be accounted for mainly by his fascinating specific details, which he obviously turned up through exhaustive research. This brief excerpt, for example, tells us specifically how Spartan boys were raised and trained, regaling us with facts about how their classes were organized, how and where they slept, and what was expected of them as they matured. We learn that they went around naked in public, that they slept on rushes, and that they were shunned for

cowardice. Durant's details, though plentiful and enlightening, are also accessible because of his straightforward, clear writing style. Notice that the excerpt moves smoothly and quickly and doesn't become bogged down for an instant—obviously Durant had an editor's eye for pacing as well.

4. In two asides, he implicitly contrasts the rearing and training of Spartan boys with the way their counterparts in Athens were treated. The significance of these asides, of course, lies in the fact the Sparta and Athens were fierce rivals, often at loggerheads and sometimes at war.

5. The author occasionally includes an unfamiliar Spartan word but immediately follows it with a parenthetical definition. For example, in paragraph 2 we are told that the boys were enrolled in a military and scholastic class under a *paidonomos*, which is defined in an aside as a "manager of boys." In paragraph 7 we are also informed that the Spartan word for marriage was *harpadzein*, and told that it meant "to seize." The author includes such words to add a flavor of realism or verisimilitude to the writing, especially important in a history of a people long gone from the earth. Such words added to the specific details make the author's story of Spartan civilization seem convincing.

Answers to Questions About the Issues

1. Allow for open discussion. Certainly, the fact that homosexuality was encouraged among Spartan hoplites, who were renowned as the fiercest fighters in ancient times, says something about the prejudices evident in the arguments that homosexuals are unfit for military service.

2. The lawgivers encouraged only a minimal literacy among the citizens probably because they feared the contamination of books that might suggest to the hapless Spartans another freer and less draconian way of life such as the Athenians enjoyed.

3. Allow for open discussion. High on the list of characteristics in Spartan society people of our own time would find especially abhorrent is the practice of eugenics, where deformed or weak children were thrown from a cliff. We think also that most people would find repugnant the idea of sharing their wives with stronger more able-bodied men for the sake of breeding haler or vigorous offspring.

4. The logical answer that he was being punished not for the crime, but for being caught committing it. One imagines that the punishment was to inculcate a sense not of morality, but of stealth.

5. Allow for open discussion. Intellect without character, history teaches, is often a more dangerous combination than character without intellect.

Consumer Reports *Used Cars: Finding a Good Buy* (pp. 352-57)

Answers to Questions About the Facts

1. See paragraph 2. The editors say that buying a used car makes good economic sense because of the rapid depreciation to which new cars are subject during the first three years.
2. The editors say that conservative car models, what they call "small and medium-sized sedans" generally make the best used cars because they are "most likely to have been driven responsibly and maintained prudently during their first tour of ownership. They also give a vote of confidence to station wagons "especially those in the lower trim lines."
3. See paragraph 7. New-car dealers are likely to charge higher prices for their used cars, say the editors, because they warranty what they sell and have the service facilities to back it up. Consequently, this protection is factored into the new-car dealers' price.
4. See paragraph 8. The article suggests that established service stations that sell cars on the side may be a responsible source of used cars because they have a reputation to protect.
5. See paragraph 12. The primary benefit of buying a used car from a private seller is a lower price since the individual does not have to factor in the possible costs of extending a warranty on the car and of backing it up. The major risk is that if something goes wrong with the car, you're on your own.

Answers to Questions About the Strategies

1. The underlying logic is this: the tests suggested are divided into two main parts--tests performed while the vehicle is parked and tests performed while the vehicle is being driven. First, the article suggests checking visually for defects and trouble signs that can be observed in the parked car during the initial walk-around. For example, the first thing suggested is a check for fluid leaks by looking under the car; the second, a check for signs of rusting; the third, a check for signs of tire wear, followed by a test for signs of a suspicious and telltale bounce in the suspension. Second, the article suggests a series of tests to be performed while the car in being

test-driven. These tests are of steering, braking, engine performance, transmission slippage, and overall comfort in the ride.

2. We ask this question because it has been pointed out to us that while magazine writers use heads to make major transitions, students generally cannot and do not because of the traditional essay form. This article typically uses bigger heads for major transitions, such as for example, the heading, "What to check on the road," and smaller so-called "be" heads for lesser transitions, such as the heads used to list "Steering," "Engine," "Transmission," "Brakes," "Exhaust," and "Comfort and quiet." A student writer, on the other hand, who cannot use these heads because they are implicitly not part of the traditional essay format, would merely have to use a transition sentence such as, "To check the brakes of the car," or "When checking the transmission" and so on.

3. The major assumption behind this article is that shopping for and buying a used car exposes the buyer to a high risk of deception and trickery. Given this premise, the article then regales us with tactics we can use to ferret out the lemons from the good buys. Indeed, as the writers tell us at the outset, this is an "imperfect world." People turn back odometers; they try to disguise years of abuse that have been inflicted on a used car; they lie about a car's history and use.

4. The phrase, "goes on the fritz" is slang meaning to break or go bad. Many instructors object to the use of such slang in freshman essays even though it is quite widespread in magazine writing.

5. They are both transition paragraphs. We occasionally like to point out to students how professional writers judiciously use paragraphs to make major transitions. It has been our experience that students only rarely use transition paragraphs.

Answers to Questions About the Issues

1. Probably the most common stereotype is that the car was owned by a little old lady who drove it weekly to church. Others abound but they share a common characteristic: in every case the previous owner is characterized as meek, mild-mannered, light-footed, and gentle on the car.

2. The popular image of the "used-car salesman" is one of a smooth-talking, sleazy, untrustworthy operator whose mission in life is to unload a lemon on the hapless buyer. Allow for other characterizations by your students. Ask your students if they have ever been pleasantly surprised to find this image utterly unfounded.

3. Allow for open discussion. Ask your students, for example, if an ethical person should volunteer negative information about a car even if the potential buyer does not specifically ask for it.

4. Allow for open discussion.

5. He or she should be assessing the ethos or character of the seller to determine whether or not that person is likely to be telling the truth about the car. If the seller is adjudged to be glib or facile, the smart buyer would walk away in a blink.

Jane Elizabeth Lemke *An Open Window on My Private World* (pp. 359-62)

Answers to Questions About the Facts

1. The author lives on one of the gulf islands of the coast of British Columbia. You might point out the area on a large map. She lives in this secluded area because she is poor and also because for her it is the proper environment for writing.
2. Because her living quarters are cramped as well as primitive—including an outhouse but no bathtub.
3. By looking out her window to the expansive view of the open bay.
4. She mentions three little girls who come to visit and a lusty German who sells her water during the rainless summer months. But in paragraph 10 she implies that she knows a number of the locals.
5. A feeling of self-sufficiency because other sources were not reliable.

Answers to Questions About the Strategies

1. The title hints at two major points developed in the essay: the open vistas seen through her window and the private nature of her existence.
2. The author does not provide a precise step by step schedule of her daily activities; yet, she gives us a clear idea of a typical day—(1) mornings: working at her writing until noon, (2) afternoons: mixing play and chores, such as exploring one of the beaches, reading, writing letters, sewing, cutting wood, paying close attention to the wildlife around her, visiting with people, and having dinner, (3) evenings: writing, playing music on her stereo, looking out into the darkness to reflect and dream, taking her sponge bath, taking one last trip to the outhouse, turning off the stove, and slipping into bed for the night.
3. Her style conveys her deep love for the intense beauties and riches of nature. The poetic details she provides add a touch of graceful loveliness. See paragraphs 3, 13, 14, and 18 for specific examples.
4. She uses a simile that compares her walks through the forest on a rainy day to stepping into an Eliot Porter photograph. For those

acquainted with Porter's magnificent photographs of U.S. landscapes—with every detail and outline recorded, including light and shadow play—the simile provides a vivid view of what she sees.

5. The final sentence is also the last step of the day, giving finality to the process analysis while repeating the main point, which is that the author considers her living quarters supremely beautiful and satisfying.

Answers to Questions About the Issues

1. The economic condition of authors is not nearly so important as their dedication to writing. Like most other artists, they have been poor more often than rich, but certainly many writers have come from comfortable and even luxurious backgrounds. Moreover, many writers started poor and ended rich. Some allowed wealth to stifle their art, and others simply squandered their money on "wine, women, and song," until they ended on welfare or in the gutter. What seems consistent about all great writers is dedication to their writing. Money or lack of it makes little difference as long as enough money exists to keep a roof over their heads and food in their stomachs.

2. Allow students to debate the issue of cutting down trees for heat and of filling the air with smoke—taking into consideration the author's isolated circumstances.

3. Many researchers have studied the environments of noted writers; however, no one environment has been viewed as superior. The truth is that some writers love to write in rooms filled with smoke and noise whereas other writers, like Lemke, prefer writing in complete isolation. Have students provide their personal perspectives.

4. The picture of the Scottish bagpiper on a cliff overlooking the ocean, playing "Amazing Grace" in the moonlight at midnight on New Year's Eve is deeply moving. We believe such a moment should cause all readers to pause quietly and think of the vastness of the universe, of the passing of time, and of the enormous beauty in nature.

5. Before having students give their individual interpretations, you might make sure that they understand that the original Buddha (Prince Siddhartha Gautama), according to legend, spent his youth in great luxury as a prince. But in his twenty-ninth year he set out to see the world and was struck by the inescapability of suffering and death. Under a pipal tree at full moon he is said to have attained enlightenment in the form of "four noble truths" and "the eightfold path." The point of the quotation is that no matter how

enlightened you become, you must never think you are too good for humble work.

Donald Barthelme *Some of Us Had Been Threatening Our Friend Colby* (pp. 364-67)

Answers to Questions About the Facts

1. Ten friends are present, including the author and Colby himself: The author, Colby,. Howard, Hugh, Magnus, Tomas, Victor, Harry, Paul, and Hank. Since this hanging is to represent a communal event, consensus must be sought among all of the participants.
2. We are merely informed that Colby has "gone too far"; however, we are never told how, where, when, or under what circumstances he had gone too far. At the end of the story we are still left to wonder.
3. Because hanging doubtlessly is against the law, and the authorities would interfere with the event if they found out that it was to be a hanging. The narrator reassures Hugh by telling him that regardless of the legality or nonlegality of the hanging, they had a perfect moral right to perform it because the culprit had "gone too far.
4. First, choose the music; second, choose and word the printed invitations and decide on whether or not to serve drinks; third, procure a gibbet; fourth, arrange for limousine transportation; fifth, get a hangman; sixth, plan Colby's drop, deciding on a rope versus a wire and a stool versus a ball.
5. The look of gratitude Colby gave the author when he supported a rope rather than a wire hanging and the fact that since Colby's hanging, no one had gone too far.

Answers to Questions About the Strategies

1. The tone is completely ironic; in other words, it is casual, matter-of-fact, and even trite whereas the subject of the essay is horrifying and shocking when we realize that a young man is being hanged—with casual planning as if hanging were in the same social league as a wedding, a birthday party, or a reception honoring someone. It is the disparity between the tone and the event that makes the tone ironic.
2. At the beginning the narrator presents Colby's increasingly bad behavior, ending in "going too far" and at the end Colby's crime has been fittingly punished, with the result that no one since Colby has gone too far. In other words, the story comes full circle.

3. This is a step-by-step process, which in itself indicates the passing of time. The author stresses the process with certain guidepost phrases, such as " The next item of business" (paragraph 3), "At this point" (paragraph 5), "Then the question of the hangman came up" (paragraph 6), "At the mention of 'wire,' Hank . . . . suddenly spoke up," (paragraph 7), ". . . on the day of the event" (paragraph 8) .
4. The concern about what kind of music to have, what kinds of invitations to send out, what drinks to serve, where to be hanged (*cf.* where to take the vows), how many limousines to have, how to make the event run smoothly and have it be effective.
5. Most of the dialogue is indirect; that is, the author avoids quoting the participants. Notice, for instance, the opening paragraph: "We asked him what sort of music he would like played at the hanging. He said he'd think about it but it would take him a while to decide. I pointed out that we'd have to know so on..." This kind of indirect conversation creates a certain distance between the characters and the subject discussed; it also avoids intense emotion, such as might be appropriate if actual words of the participants were quoted.

Answers to Questions About the Issues

1. The point of view is what literary critics call "absurdist"— view that life is ridiculous because anything can happen at any time, and no one is in charge of human destiny. In such a world, a community could well decide to hang one of its members for an undefined crime and the victim might even go along with the hanging. The reaction to typically absurdist literature is shock and sadness, combined with laughter. Much of modern literature seems to see life from the absurdist angle--perhaps because the Christian God of providence has given way to science and its rather unpredictable destinies. One laughs to escape despair, an act often described as black humor.
2. One of the common flaws of tragic characters in classic drama was *hubris,* the flaw of excessive pride (e.g. Oedipus, Macbeth, Othello). Such characters would strive for too much power, were excessively envious, or could not control their tempers. AS a result, they usually forfeited their lives by being murdered or by committing suicide.
3. Most research indicates that capital punishment is not a deterrent to crime. For instance, the crime of murder is usually committed in great anger and against someone in the family or close to the murderer. Moreover, Mafia-type murderers believe (and rightly so) that they will never be caught; thus , capital punishment does not deter them either.

4. Students should share their individual reactions. It seems to us that one message is the tragic isolation of individuals in a society where no one is closed to anyone else and where people have become desensitized to violence and find it Impossible to love each other and to be intimate such each other. Ink such a world, the most heartless act, such as a hanging, would symbolically become trite and could be handled with extreme casualness.
5. The story seems to accept tradition unquestioningly. Is a person goes too far, that person is hanged. The tradition is never questioned and refuted. It becomes merely a question of following the tradition with taste and proper protocol.

Kenneth Patchen *How to Be an Army* (pp. 368-69)

Answers to Questions About the Facts

1. Here is a sample answer: "To assemble a proper army to wage war, one needs uniforms, rations, a national flag, the toughness to put up with filthy conditions, military arms, trenches, determination, discipline, the willingness to spill much blood, generals to lead the war, and a patriotic readiness to die in the belief that one's side is right. "
2. Because boots are an important part of the military uniform. Probably the poet was thinking of the kind of combat that requires soldiers to march long distances or to march in military parades goose-step style, kicking up their polished boots.
3. The meaning is ambiguous, as poetry often is; nonetheless, one possible interpretation is that in most wars, the odds are uneven (the equation being approximately 1 to 2), with one side mightier than the other, thus creating inevitable bloodshed

Answers to Questions About the Strategies

1. Various answers apply. We suggest that the author may be saying that even a child can see the evils of war when they are realistically and truthfully presented.
2. The irony is that no matter how strongly one side believes in its cause, the war still results in many graveyards, where the soldiers must be buried, as represented by the lines of crosses.
3. He simply enlarges the print, making the word or concept stand out boldly. Examples are the title and the equation. Have students discuss their reaction to the strategy. Some may indicate that they consider the strategy a simpleminded, obvious ploy.

1. This is a question that reaches straight to students' personal philosophies and beliefs. Encourage honest introspection. You might use recent wars and the conflicts that caused them as a testing ground for the question. For instance, you might ask if the oil in Kuwait was enough reason for them to be willing to fight in a war with Iraq.
2. Allow for open discussion on this point. We suggest that all of them are necessary, but that when the participants are inflamed with fervor or fanaticism, they have an enhanced chance of winning, given most circumstances of war. For instance, during the medieval crusades, religious fervor moved soldiers to feats of heroism and sacrifice in order to win back the holy city of Jerusalem at all costs.
3. The obvious missing ingredient is the atomic bomb with its capacity to destroy the entire world.

Lynn Z. Bloom *Teaching College English as a Woman* (pp. 372-80)

Answers to Questions About the Facts

1. Because her first job following her PhD was part-time instruction at a distinguished midwestern university, where she never expressed an original opinion of her own about literature, but merely quoted the opinion of noted male critics.
2. She accuses him of gender bias because he scolded her for writing a paper implying that the Eve of Milton's *Paradise Lost* had some virtues. She also accuses him of not bothering to finish reading her paper.
3. Because having no office was symbolic of the status the English Department had assigned to her. She was actually forced to sit on the floor next to the litter box of her office mate's cat, held captive in the office.
4. They were four male-tenured faculty members who made it their mission to stifle the author's voice in the English Department-- accusing her of being more interested in teaching students how to write than in literary criticism and of promoting her own career through her published writings.
5. She wanted them to understand the difference between male love and male violence and she wanted the females in her class to stand up to male domination through violence.

Answers to Questions About the Strategies

1. Whereas the title is the kind typically found in an English journal, the inside headings are reminders of a play or musical performance—beginning with the "Prologue" and ending with a "coda." Titles like "My Job as Ventriloquist's Dummy" or "on the Floor with the Kitty Litter" belong more in a theatrical comedy than in an English journal. By using these unusual headings, the author captivates our interest and creates a sense of irony.

2. The author builds up suspense and emotion, ending with the dramatic, "Ultimately I didn't count." In other words, no matter how hard she worked and regardless of the quality of her work, she was dismissed—presumably because she was a woman.

3. Allow students to discuss the situation of having the author sit on the floor next to the litter box of her office mate's cat. One purpose served is to crystallize in the reader's mind the humiliation caused when a college teacher has to resort to sitting on the floor instead of having a decent office desk with telephone, computer system, book case, stationery, and so forth. The author states (paragraph 11) that she was treated like an illegal alien.

4. The term "gang of four" is remindful of the radical communists who surrounded Mao Tse-tung's widow, Chang Ch'ing, and tried to wield power in China following Mao's death. The term connotes an unwillingness to allow new forces to shape the future of an institution; it connotes the desire to see an in-group maintain ultimate authority.

5. She paces her narration well, passing over all incidents of the family camping trip and of the particular stormy evening, except for the author's trek to the shower. At that point she begins to supply vivid details and a blow-by-blow description of what happened, building up suspense until she escapes naked into the corridor of the hostel. She builds up terror by using descriptive passages such as "As I groped for a light switch in the pitch black room, it struck me as odd that the lights were off at night in a public building. The room was dead silent, not even a faucet was dripping." The author's use of spoken passages also adds to the intrigue of the story.

Answers to Questions About the Issues

1. Have students discuss this question. We suspect that situations in colleges and universities across the nation vary. We do believe that women in education have made gigantic strides toward equality with men in the areas of rank, payment, class assignments, and

authority in colleges and universities. Especially on the undergraduate level, women outnumber men at some institutions. They continue to lag behind in top positions, such as those of deans, vice-presidents, presidents, and chancellors. In our experience, the real underdog of college teaching is the unfortunate part-time faculty member—male or female—who must teach at three or four different institutions in order to make a paltry living—without retirement or medical benefits.

2. She certainly reflects a deep love for teaching, for writing, and for literature. When a teacher loves her job and the subject she teaches, that devotion is bound to express itself in the classroom. The author claims that she argued and joked with her students and that the classroom experience was fun. She also demonstrates courage and tenacity, valuable characteristics of a teacher. On the negative side, she reveals a touch of paranoia. One wonders if she was really as persecuted as she felt she was.

3. Here are some questions to ask students:
   1. Should tenure be based on time served? How?
   2. If quality should be involved in tenure, how should it be assessed? What standards should be used?
   3. Once a teacher has been granted tenure, how can continued excellence be assured?

4. How should students be involved in an instructor's tenure?

4. Here are the usual arguments given in favor of teacher assistants:
   1. They save the university money.
   2. They lift the burden of tedious, repetitive teaching from the shoulders of full-time professors, allowing them more time for research, graduate seminars, or upper-division lecture preparation.
   3. They understand the students' problems, being students themselves.

5. The two incidents stress the thesis that a female teacher at the university must be strong in order to survive and make her mark.

William Zinsser *The Right to Fail* (pp. 382-84)

Answers to Questions About the Facts

1. Our selection is the end sentence of paragraph 2: "For the young, dropping out is often a way of dropping in. "
2. The rebels and the conformers. Zinsser's sympathy is with the rebels.

3.   He uses examples of successes who once suffered conspicuous failures, and his method provides gritty details needed to support his thesis. He tells us stories of Thomas Hoving, of Fred Zinnemann, and of Richard Brooks.
4.   Paragraph 9. It is necessary lest his essay be taken as a defense of idleness or aimlessness, which it is not. Failure in Zinsser's philosophy is a necessary part of the journey to success. It is not the end itself, but the means to an end.

Answers to Questions About the Strategies

1.   The title asserts an unusual right. The reader is accustomed to dealing with "the right to vote," or the "right to pursue happiness," or the "right to succeed, " but failure is traditionally seen as something to avoid at all costs; thus the irony of the title will compel attention.
2.   Qualifying and setting limits make the argument seem reasonable rather than irrational. Without the qualifications and limits, Zinsser would appear to be arguing for failure in all circumstances, an outlandish opinion. Instead, he qualifies his argument by acknowledging that not everyone should drop out of college and that some failure may be due to laziness or irresponsibility. Moreover, he limits his examples to people who succeeded despite failure.
3.   In the 1960s Holden Caulfield became a prototype of the young generation of students who felt that those in charge of schools and jobs were phonies incapable of the slightest understanding of youth's sensitivities or aspirations.
4.   For Zinsser, a *dropout* is a person trying to succeed on his own terms by maintaining his individual vision. In contrast, society considers the *dropout* a "fink"; that is, a person who undermines or flouts the standards and values of the educational establishment.

Answers to Questions About the Issues

1.   One could argue either side successfully. On the one hand, people like Jesus of Nazareth, Galileo Galilei, and Joan of Arc were persecuted; on the other hand, people like Mahatma Gandhi, Will Rogers, and Theodore Roosevelt were admired.
2.   Allow for individual responses to this question.
3.   Although it is true that many students need to mature by sidestepping college or dropping out for a while before they become serious about their studies, by the time they decide to come back to college, much valuable time has passed and they are forced to spend long hours catching up to those who took the more direct route of staying in college. We often hear the following lament

from our returning students: "I wish I had stayed in college; I would be through by now." Or, "My writing skills are really rusty because I've been out of college for so long. " Or, "I am filled with anxiety about succeeding in this course; I didn't want to go to college, but now that I do, I'm having to worry about whether I am capable." We rarely hear students state that they are sorry they didn't drop out of college for a while.
4. Have the students make up their own individual lists; then read them to the class.
5. Allow for varying views on this question.

Chapter Seven EXPLAINING: Illustration and Definition

Caskie Stinnett *Farewell, My Unlovely* (pp. 393-97)

Answers to Questions About the Facts

1. The fact that he felt so little sadness about leaving a city in which he had lived for ten years.
2. He yearns for them to possess a nature that could be stimulated by something.
3. The sheer meanness associated with it.
4. He says that it is totally controlled by the labor unions.
5. The occasional loveliness of the city, the beautiful girls, the exhilarating tempo of the city's life.

Answers to Questions About the Strategies

1. He uses the detail about Naples and Bombay being dirtier than New York and about his friend with flawless taste who lives in Tangiers, which is far dirtier than New York.
2. "This" refers of course to the man dropping the empty carton on the ground when he could just as easily have used the litter can. The sentence is a transitional sentence. Since the antecedent of the pronoun is in the preceding paragraph, readers automatically link both paragraphs together as they read.
3. The contrast is between the behavior of the author's dog and the passive behavior of the people of New York. The irony is in the author's wish that New Yorkers would behave more like his dog.
4. With the introductory remark, "I recall."

5. It is clear from the context of the paragraph that the three incidents mentioned are intended as examples of the terrible meanness of New York's crimes.

Answers to Questions About the Issues

1. Here are some facts in defense of New York (allow students to suggest their own):
   a. The city is one of the world's strongholds of culture. In support of this truth, one need only cite such institutions as the Metropolitan Museum of Art, the Museum of Modern Art, the Guggenheim Museum, the Frick Collection, the Whitney Museum of American Art, the Museum of Primitive Art, and the American Museum of Natural History. New York City is also the home of the Lincoln Center for Performing Arts, which houses the famous Metropolitan Opera Company, the New York Philharmonic-Symphony Orchestra, the New York City Ballet, the New York City Opera, the Julliard School, and the Vivian Beaumont Theatre and Library Building. Some of the world's most outstanding structures are in New York: the Empire State Building, the World Trade Center Buildings, Trinity Church, St. Paul's Chapel, Saint Patrick's Cathedral, the Cathedral of Saint John the Divine, Grant's Tomb.
   b. The city practically controls the world's finances through its influential business activities on Wall Street.
   c. New York Harbor is one of the world's leading ports.
   d. New York supports the education of its citizens. It has one of the world's most successful public school systems, including the City University of New York with its nine colleges. The New York Public Library, a free library supported by heavy private endowments, is known internationally.

   This list is at best partial.
2. Allow for creative suggestions on the part of students. Here are a few ideas to discuss:
   a. Forming neighborhood watches.
   b. Stressing the importance of parents getting involved in their children's school activities in order to get acquainted with their neighbors.
   c. Mounting public relations campaigns that stress compassion and altruism in city life.
   d. Offering activities that enrich one's spiritual life, such as church attendance.
3. Allow students to jog their memories for appropriate examples. Encourage them to present cases involving personal acquaintances.
4. Allow for individual expression.

5.   Allow for individual answers.

John Leo *Mirror, Mirror, on the Wall* (pp. 398-400)

Answers to Questions About the Facts

1.   Concerned with fertility, primitive man idealized ample women.
2.   They considered fair-haired women exotic, and admired what the author calls "magnificent mammaries."
3.   Evolutionary selection caused by male preference for big-breasted women.
4.   The wan, cadaverous look.
5.   A rebellion against male dominance, and a reluctance to engage in childbearing.

Answers to Questions About the Strategies

1.   "That notions of what is most attractive do vary with each age and culture." This idea is hinted at in the first paragraph, and plainly stated at the beginning of the second.
2.   Allusions.
3.   That the Greeks had a high regard for women with large breasts.
4.   It adds a note of authority to his assertions.
5.   With examples drawn from the Middle Ages and from the sixteenth century.

Answers to Questions About the Issues

1.   An anthropologized world is a world in which the bonds of human society have been studied and categorized from the historical and physical point of view in order to see how various cultures have developed. The value of anthropology lies in its ability to link up with other sciences, such as archaeology, psychology, and linguistics, to better understand the deep-rooted myths and traditions of various people, even in nonliterate times.
2.   Allow for individual answers to this question.
3.   Allow for varying opinions on this question. Some critics of today's aerobics craze have stated that the lean and muscular look is not as sensual as a softer, more curvaceous body.
4.   Aristotle argued that true beauty must reflect the ideals of harmony, balance, and radiance. He believed that beauty in art could be judged by these objective standards.

5. Certainly our American society has restored the view of women as sexual beings. In fact, one might argue that we are living in an age where sexual freedom has gone too far, leading to a corrosion of the family unit and to life-threatening sexual diseases.

Lewis Thomas, M.D. *On Natural Death* (pp. 402-04)

Answers to Questions About the Facts

1. They are all process books, telling their readers how to do something easily, efficiently, and well. One presumes that in a society as busy and occupied as ours, every minute must be accounted for and therefore books on how to accomplish a process effectively with minimum worry would become immensely popular.
2. These instructions annul the naturalness of the death process, turning it into a technique that can be learned so that the task is accomplished gracefully.
3. The elm tree that died of blight and the field mouse killed by a household cat. The elm exemplifies the death of a plant that has no pain receptors, whereas the mouse exemplifies the death of a creature capable of sensing pain. In his argument the author makes little distinction between the two because he suggests that at the point of death neither victim feels actual pain.
4. First the example of Montaigne, and then the example of the soldiers on Okinawa during World War II. In both cases the subjects were mortally wounded, but none suffered great physical pain as they neared death. Montaigne recovered whereas the soldiers died.
5. He feels that it is an expertly-designed natural function.

Answers to Questions About the Strategies

1. It is stated in the final sentence of the paragraph-a strategic placement, leaving the reader with a sense of peace about the process of dying. If, for instance, the author had closed with the examples of the tree, mouse, or soldiers, we might have felt sad and not completely comforted.
2. An audience of educated readers, but not necessarily scientifically trained. The author's style is lucid, free from clutter, and developed through examples that even a child could understand. What keeps the essay from being naive or simpleminded is the fact that the author is an eminent scientist who knows the complex anatomical as well as medical facts about dying. Yet, he chooses to see the process in simple and essential terms.

3. In paragraph 5, he begins with a reference to "that mouse," which is the topic of paragraph 4; thus, the reader knows that the topic of paragraph 5 is still the field mouse of paragraph 4.
4. Allow for differing answers on that point. We suggest that the scientific terms (*peptide hormones, hypothalamus, pituitary gland, endorphins, pharmalogic properties*) do give some weight to the suggestion, lifting it out of the realm of purely imaginary speculation.
5. Thoughtful students will perceive that appropriate examples are an excellent technique for simplifying or clarifying a complex subject. They are probably the most common strategy of writers attempting to explain something or make a point. Stress to students that when they use examples in their own essays, they must make sure that, like those used by Lewis Thomas, the examples are relevant and properly introduced.

Answers to Questions About the Issues

1. Both of these questions require a personal reaction from students. Although the essay may not assuage our typical anxieties and questionings about death, it certainly provides a reassuring tone from a scientist who obviously knows a great deal about the subject, having no doubt watched many people die during his career as a physician.
2. Allow students to answer these questions freely, sharing thoughts and specific death scenes. Of course, if the discussion becomes ghoulish or maudlin, move on to a more pleasant approach.
3. Allow students to explain themselves individually.
4. Actually, it may take more courage to face death without having any hope of future existence. History is replete with accounts of human beings who did not profess a belief in any kind of afterlife, but died bravely. It does seem that people with a deep faith in God and heaven can look at death with more philosophical serenity than can those who think of death as simply a biological process that ends all.
5. An example of a good death is the death of an aged person who has led an exemplary life, filled with satisfying accomplishments. An example of a terrible death is the death of a murderer condemned to death in the electric chair of a prison.

Adrienne Rich *Living in Sin* (pp. 406-07)

Answers to Questions About the Facts

1. Like many lovers caught up in the heat of making love, the woman gives no thought to the demands of daily life that follow a passionate sex encounter-making the bed, tidying up, keeping the house clean- thinking it a departure from the traditional way of treating love to even consider such unromantic matters. Making love is all-consuming until the next morning.
2. The whole romantic scene is transformed by reality: the steps squeak as the milkman noisily ascends them to deliver the milk; scraps of cheese and empty wine bottles lie on the table while a cockroach or some other critter faces the woman.
3. The man casually rises and leaves to go buy a pack of cigarettes while the woman is left to straighten up the mess left by last night's love orgy.

Answers to Questions About the Strategies

1. The line should read "She had not thought that. . . ." This grammatical ellipsis creates ambiguity and subtlety of meaning, thus increasing the sense of delight created by the poem.
2. The woman's, because she is the one whose romantic views make it difficult for her to deal with reality whereas the man seems to be more casual and thus less affected by the ugly picture of passion's aftermath.
3. First, he is the actual milkman ascending the stairs to deliver his products; second, he serves as a simile for the inevitability of dawn arriving to force the woman back to reality with its unromantic daily chores.
4. Because *sepulchral* means "suggestive of the grave," the word adds an unpleasantly dark connotation to the description of the three empty wine bottles, as if they were dead and should be buried.

Answers to Questions About the Issues

1. The poet is supporting the well-known saying that "love is blind" and that the real workaday world will inevitably reassert itself once the passion of love has been exhausted.
2. The contrast between the romance of the scene when the noisy pipes, the cat stalking a mouse near the shawl-draped piano, and the intimate snack of cheese, pears, and wine are part of the

97

wonderful intimacy the man and woman are experiencing, and the scene the next morning when those same images contribute to a sense of revulsion.

3. Once the woman has cleaned up the studio, she is ready for another passionate session of love-making; however, the reader senses that with each experience, the romance will lessen and reality will intrude until the passion vanishes completely.

4. Allow students to present individual views on this question. We suggest that it has little to do with love, which means caring for an individual and planning life goals together. The image here is mostly of sexual lust bolstered by trite symbols of romance.

John Henry Newman *On Liberal Knowledge* (pp. 411-13)

Answers to Questions About the Facts

1. According to Newman, knowledge must be impregnated by reason. When knowledge is so impregnated, it is like a fertilized egg; it grows and gives birth to either a practical art or simply a philosophic attitude. The practical art is called "useful knowledge," whereas the philosophic attitude is called "liberal knowledge."

2. Newman excludes from liberal knowledge all education that leads either to specific facts, practical arts, or mechanical processes.

3. According to Newman, liberal knowledge is general knowledge-the comprehension of broad outlines rather than specific tangible data. It is the kind of knowledge that may never bring results such as a work of art or a cured disease. It is knowledge for the sake of knowledge, no other purpose.

4. Various answers are possible. Examples:
    a. philosophy of history = liberal knowledge
    b. advanced dress design = useful knowledge
    c. Shakespeare = liberal knowledge
    d. journalism = useful knowledge
    e. ballet = useful knowledge
    f. European civilization = liberal knowledge

5. Because one is instructed in the useful arts, but one is educated to a state or condition of the mind. The university is properly a place of education, not instruction, because it promotes the kind of knowledge that acts on mental nature and forms character. Have your students discuss whether Newman's kind of education should be the sole responsibility of the university.

Answers to Questions About the Strategies

1. Newman's paragraphs are long; his sentences are complex; his ideas are abstract.
2. Newman leads the reader from point to point and is careful to repeat key words. Also, he uses transitional signal expressions, such as "then," "but," "In one case . . . in the other. . . ." He summarizes what he has said, before going on to the next idea, as: "You see, then, here are two methods of Education; the end of the one is to be philosophical, of the other to be mechanical. "
3. The allusion does not break the unity of the paragraph, since it is Newman's purpose to define liberal knowledge. One way to define is by saying what the term is not. According to Newman, liberal knowledge is completely different from the kind of response to sensations expressed by brute animals. It is on a much higher plane because it is intellectual: it grasps what it perceives; it takes a view of things; it reasons upon what it sees.
4. See the last two sentences of paragraph 1.

Answers to Questions About the Issues

1. Indeed, knowledge is perhaps the most powerful force in any society. In fact, without knowledge, a society would remain on the level of brutes. Because of the power inherent in knowledge, every king, emperor, or president in history has surrounded himself with a circle of specialists to advise him—magistrates, ministers, cabinet members. In a peace-seeking world, knowledge must, of course, be accompanied by a strong sense of responsibility. Consider, for example, what would happen if some brilliant but evil person learned how to detonate an atomic bomb, or how to take over a television news broadcast, or how to write an influential book.
2. For an excellent answer to this question, read Alan Simpson's "Marks of an Educated Man," pp. 202-07.
3. Encourage students to be specific in their descriptions of personal acquaintances whom they consider "educated. " One of the editors of this book has enormous respect for a research perinatologist, who spends most of his waking hours doing research on the human fetus but still makes time to read Victorian novels, attend philharmonic concerts, visit art galleries, and discuss philosophical issues. This scientist's emphasis on the liberal arts keeps him in touch with the nitty-gritty aspects of the human predicament—sorrow, doubt, fear, joy, love, and so forth. Without this influence of the liberal arts, he might well be a one-sided thinker.

4. Art for art's sake, or beauty for beauty's sake. In other words, art is not of necessity the strict imitation of nature. It need not have a specific purpose or follow specific rules, but rather can exist simply as art, to be loved merely because it is there.
5. This is a position only sophistical students will want to attempt to take. They probably will argue that philosophical questions can never be answered satisfactorily and are, therefore, a waste of mental energy; that studying literature, while pleasant, consumes too much time that can be used in more lucrative pursuits; and that the fine arts in general can be enjoyed only by the aristocratic elements of society whereas the poor are forced to spend all of their time finding food and shelter.

Pico Iyer *In Praise of the Humble Comma* (pp. 414-17)

Answers to Questions About the Facts

1. Punctuation is defined several times throughout the essay:
   "Punctuation marks are the road signs placed along the highway of our communication . . . . " (paragraph 2)
   "Punctuation . . . is a civic prop, a pillar that holds society upright. " (paragraph 3)
   "Punctuation thus becomes the signature of cultures. " (paragraph 4)
   "Punctuation is the notation in the sheet music of our words. . . ." (paragraph 5)
   "Punctuation, then, is a matter of care." (paragraph 9)
   Allow students to indicate their individual preferences in response to the second part of the question. We prefer the definition of road signs because it stresses the practical aspects of punctuation as a means of establishing continuity and clarity in written communication.
2. The comma falls under the author's definitions of punctuation in general. Moreover, he clearly establishes the function of the comma when he indicates that the comma allows us to take a breath (paragraph 1), that it tells us to "slow down," (paragraph 2), that it separates items (paragraph 2), that it gives us "breadth and heft and depth," that it "catches the general drift of the mind in thought." We are certainly not left in doubt as to what a comma is supposed to do.
3. He means that every culture establishes certain punctuation marks as expositions of its feelings, social attitudes, and political leanings.
4. Like notations on a piece of sheet music, punctuation tells the reader when to pause, when to speed up, when to become excited,

and when to take a breath—thus creating feelings in the written work.

5.   Without commas, writing would reflect a heavy, stomping rhythm void of fine nuances and shades of meaning.

Answers to Questions About the Strategies

1.   He views the comma as the most artistic facet of punctuation. In other words, to use commas appropriately requires a sense of style and rhythm in addition to having a clear idea to express.

2.   In a sense, Iyer's style is ironic because punctuation, like all other aspects of grammar, is usually considered mundane, arid, and uninteresting. But here Iyer uses a poetic style with poetic images to describe and define punctuation. Have students point out some specific examples of poetic images. Here are four: "Punctuation . . . is a civic prop, a pillar that holds society upright." (paragraph 3) "A run-on sentence, its phrases piling up without division, is as unsightly as a sink piled high with dirty dishes." (paragraph 3) "Punctuation is the notation in the sheet music of our words...." (paragraph 5) "Popping in a comma can be like slipping on the necklace that gives an outfit quiet elegance...." (paragraph 7)

3.   The tone is ironic, because as the essay progresses, we find that the comma is an essential part of written communication and certainly the mark requiring the most artistic control. In other words, the comma may seem humble, but it is important.

4.   He uses the technique of coming full circle. He began his essay by alluding to the gods and closes it by coming back to them. This technique is often used by writers of short essays because it brings the essay to a nice, neat finality-like closing up a circle.

5.   At the beginning of paragraph 6, he summarizes the meaning of paragraph 5, an excellent way of assuring coherence between paragraphs.

Answers to Questions About the Issues

1.   Students will doubtless have differing opinions on the subject. We suggest that our culture is divided into various approaches to punctuation. We have the sophisticated literati who use punctuation correctly as well as artistically; then we have people who use punctuation more or less according to the grammatical rules taught them in elementary and high school; but then we have the vast majority of citizens who have no clue about how to punctuate properly. It is this large mass that colleges are trying to remediate, but it is an extremely difficult task. Consequently, much writing today is confused, meaningless, and dull.

2. Allow students to express themselves individually on this question. Probably, the commas will be cited by most students as the most difficult mark to use correctly.
3. These questions require students to think for themselves. Our contention is that the writers mentioned--James Joyce and e.e. cummings--knew perfectly well how to punctuate according to grammatical rules, and only after they had mastered the basics did they feel free to ignore them--just as modern painters and musicians can invent new styles once they have mastered the fundamental techniques of their arts.
4. A thorough discussion of this question should conclude that careful writing is the basis of careful scholarship and leads to excellence in most professions.
5. Students should be amused by this exercise. In case no one can think of a sentence to start the exercise, here are three obvious ones: "Unfortunately, we must deny your loan. " Or, "Congress has declared war. " Or, "I am simply not in love with you. " Many other examples should come to mind

Gilbert Highet *Kitsch* (pp. 418-26)

Answers to Questions About the Facts

1. Highet gives a definition of *kitsch* in paragraph 3: ". . . it means vulgar showoff, and it is applied to anything that took a lot of trouble to make and is quite hideous." The rest of the question can be answered in various ways. Example: "Kitsch is anything that is ostentatious and in bad taste. The Greek ideal of elegant simplicity would be the opposite of kitsch. "

2. Highet provides the following examples of kitsch:

Paragraphs 1-2:	Items in antique shops
Paragraphs 6-7:	Excerpts from the works of Mrs. Amanda McKittrick Ros
Paragraphs 8-14:	Excerpts from the Scottish poet William McGonagall
Paragraph 15:	Lines from the poetry of Ezra Pound
Paragraph 17:	College songs, the works of Father Divine, a line from Sri Ramakrishna, Stephen Spender's "The Archibald MacLeish
Paragraph 18:	Four lines from Coleridge's address to a donkey
Paragraph 19:	Bad translations, abstract paintings, grand opera, Dr. Johnson

Paragraph 20:	Folk poetry, such as an epitaph on a man who died in a sawmill accident
Paragraph 21:	The play *Young England*
Paragraph 22:	The decorative arts, such as the statue of Atlas in Rockefeller Center. New York.

3. Ros describes the hero's black eyes as "glittering jet revolvers." Encourage students to suggest a more restrained metaphor.
4. Sample answer: McGonagall's description of the arctic landscape, replete with church spires and icy monuments, is completely fantastic, having no connection with reality. The ending of one of his Gothic ballads is utterly ridiculous; the heroine invokes Heaven's will on her wedding night. And his rhyming of "shame" with "Graham," or of "stigma" with "Digna" is glaringly amateurish.
5. The essence of kitsch is incongruity-the union of things that simply do not belong together (see paragraph 16). Have students point out the incongruity in some of the examples.

Answers to Questions About the Strategies

1. The predominant tone is ironic. Note the following examples from paragraph 6:

    (In paragraph 5 Highet has just stated that he collects kitsch in books.) "The gem of my collection is the work of the Irish novelist Mrs. Amanda McKittrick Ros. . . ." (The word *gem* is used ironically.) "Mrs. Ros had a remarkable command of rhetoric, and could coin an unforgettable phrase. She described her hero's black eyes as 'glittering jet revolvers.'" (The phrase is doubtless unforgettable because it is so horrible.)

    "I regret only that I have never seen Mrs. Ros's poetry. " (After hearing examples of her dreadful prose, we can only imagine how much worse her poetry would be.)

2. Highet uses striking figurative language throughout his essay. Much of the time it is humorous. Examples:

    | Paragraph 2: | "like illicit drugs" (This is hyperbolic.) |
    | Paragraph 6: | "sound and fury, signifying nothing" (This quotation from Shakespeare used in the context of a discussion on kitsch creates humorous incongruity.) |
    | Paragraph 7: | "conferring upon her dewy brow the laurels of concrete immortality" (Here Highet is using Mrs. Ros's own style to poke fun at her.) |

Paragraph 8:   "In his command of platitude and his disregard of melody, he was the true heir of William Wordsworth as a descriptive poet." (This allusion to Wordsworth is meant to be satirical.)

3.   Highet develops his essay by using one example after another because examples help the reader to formulate a vivid idea of what kitsch is.
4.   McGonagall's poetry is so bad that it serves not as a compliment but as an instrument of derision.

Answers to Questions About the Issues

1.   Various examples are possible. You might suggest the following as springboards for discussion: Disneyland, Christmas cards, items in souvenir shops, certain hotels in Hawaii or Las Vegas.
2.   The delight may result from the item's ability to draw attention to itself, or perhaps from the humor that is often a concomitant effect of hideousness. In paragraph 6, Highet refers to piece of writing as "revolting, but distinctive. "
3.   Lack of experience in judging art inevitably leads people to find delight in the gaudy, the garish, and the obvious rather than in subtlety and understatement. An educated eye will rarely mistake kitsch for great art.

4.   Allow for individual presentations.

5.   Poem A is entitled "Ditty" and was composed by an American poet, Ted Robinson. Poem B is entitled "Dover Beach" and was composed by the Victorian poet Matthew Arnold. To a mind trained in reading poetry, poem B is the superior poem because it is less trite, less predictable, less obvious in its rhyme and meter, and more profound than is poem A. While both poems indicate that love is the one port of peace in an otherwise stormy world, poem B delivers its message with restraint and subtlety, whereas poem A is self-evident as well as self-conscious.

Frank Deford *Cystic Fibrosis* (pp. 428-32)

Answers to Questions About the Facts

1.   See paragraph 1. Cystic fibrosis is a disease mainly of the lungs. The body produces too much mucus, which obstructs the flow of

air into the sufferer's lungs and clogs the pancreas and, in the male, the testes.

2. Eighteen.
3. The author says that their attitude is ambivalent. They admire the doctors but also associate them with pain and suffering.
4. Inhalation treatments, physical therapy, medication.
5. "I won't have to do therapy when I'm a lady, will I?" (Paragraph 16)

Answers to Questions About the Strategies

1. In exactly the same way. He places cystic fibrosis in the class of *disease*, and then proceeds to show specifically the kind of disease it is. He specifies that it attacks the lungs and disparate organs, that its killing agent is excessive mucus, and that its victims inevitably die.
2. His logical sequence is this: First, he defines the disease. Then he spends a paragraph on its agent—mucus. He then describes the spectrum of cases, ranging from the mildest to the most extreme. After that, he shows where Alex fell in this spectrum and describes the treatment regimen she had to undergo.
3. It gives a perspective from the viewpoint of the suffering child, adding a harrowing human dimension to the definition.
4. This is one of those injunctions some instructors dispense in the classroom (Don't address the reader as "you"!) but writers often ignore. In fact, by addressing the reader outright as "you" and asking him or her to understand how he felt, Deford adds a personal and touching appeal to his story. Students seldom have the sensitivity to know when overuse of the "you" becomes cloying and when it can be effective, hence the blanket injunction against all "you's."

Answers to Questions About the Issues

1. Urge students to think deeply about the implications of their answers, but encourage them to be honest.
2. Most parents of handicapped children try their utmost to educate their child to be a well-adjusted, independent person; however, in most cases the parents also reveal a natural tendency to protect the handicapped child from the ravages of a society that can often be cruel and impatient.
3. Allow for personal anecdotes.
4. We need funding for better research and we also need more adjunct instruction in the schools, especially on the elementary level. Furthermore, we should teach ourselves to be more understanding of handicapped people so that we include them in our lifestyles rather than exclude them because they seem different.

5. Probably because the disease involves pain, and a child associates pain with such common punishments as spanking, having to eat distasteful food, being forced to remain in a corner or a room alone, being humiliated, and so forth. The whole Christian religion is based on a system of painful punishment for those who commit evil.

Archibald MacLeish *Ars Poetica* (pp. 433-34)

Answers to Questions About the Facts

1. Latin writers wrote dissertations on various arts—even the art of love (Ovid's *Ars Amatoria*). The use of Latin titles has been interpreted as a sign of scholarship during much of English literary history. In this case, the title is ironic since the poem is not a scholarly analysis of the art of writing poetry and in fact rejects that approach.
2. MacLeish never gives an explicit definition of poetry. The implication is that poetry cannot be defined, only expressed. The meaning of poetry is conveyed through a series of figurative images. In other words, the author defines poetry by telling us how it works. The definition is subtle but nonetheless clear once we understand all the images.
3. The author means that poetry creates an illusion of reality, but it is not reality itself. For example, in her poem "Because I Could Not Stop for Death," Emily Dickinson describes death as a kindly gentleman calling on a lady to take her for a carriage ride. The picture is not reality in terms of commonsense perceptions, but the picture is "equal to" reality; that is, it is as good a picture of death as one can give, since death is an unknown.
4. MacLeish means that poetry is above and beyond pedantic parsing or word-by-word analysis. You have to understand it through intuition more than through reason.

Answers to Questions About the Strategies

1. Possible interpretations of the paradoxes:
   a. "palpable and mute / As a globed fruit": To the sensitive reader, a poem will be as obvious as a ripe pear or apple.
   b. "Dumb / As old medallions to the thumb": When a reader is in tune with the poem he is reading, he will extract as much meaning as a soldier extracts memories from a medal he won during wartime.

c. "Silent as the sleeve-worn stone / Of casement ledges where the moss has grown": Poems contain as much information about life as does the window ledge of an old house that has seen much living.

d. "A poem should be motionless in time / As the moon climbs": As the moon slowly but inevitably releases its enchanting glow over the landscape at night, so poetry gradually releases its meaning, enlightening the mind of the reader.

2. For most readers the images seem entirely appropriate since the empty doorway becomes symbolic of the fact that death cancels all entrances and exits in life, and the maple leaf on the ground symbolizes autumn and loneliness. In this way, the history of grief is summarized in death and loneliness. In addition, the image evokes a feeling of gloom and finality. Your students will suggest other possible images that stand for the history of grief.

3. The scene is a marshy strand by the seaside at night. In the heavens two stars are twinkling. The scene is appropriate because it is romantic, and the two stars are like two lovers who need only each other to be happy.

4. The poet uses three synonyms for *mute:* dumb, silent, wordless.

5. In the sixth and seventh stanzas the moon gives the effect of climbing imperceptibly. The repetition of the fifth stanza thus reinforces the idea that although the moon climbs slowly, it sheds more and more light. In a similar way, the meaning of the poem will dawn on the reader slowly and imperceptibly.

Answers to Questions About the Issues

1. Various answers are possible.

2. This question should challenge your students' imaginations. In the past, our students have suggested these symbols: a cross and a Bible, a tear stained lace handkerchief, a weeping willow tree standing alone by a silent lake.

3. Presumably the author is telling us that great poetry never consists of drawn-out versification that involves all kinds of unnecessary words and sound patterns. Rather, it is thought condensed to its quintessential meaning. It never thunders thoughtlessly, but instead reveals its meaning only after quiet concentration.

4. The kind of poem that best exemplifies MacLeish's view will be concrete rather than abstract. Its meaning will most likely be revealed through appropriate tropes. Perhaps MacLeish is speaking out against long poems with meanings so abstruse that the reader must ponder and ponder before they make any sense. Here is a poem that might fit MacLeish's mold:

107

To make a prairie it takes a clover
        and one bee,—
One clover, and a bee,
And revery.
The revery alone will do
If bees are few

Emily Dickinson

Stephen Chapman *The Prisoner's Dilemma* (pp. 437-43)

Answers to Questions About the Facts

1. Paragraph 8: "At least in regard to cruelty, it's not at all clear that the system of punishment that has evolved in the West is less barbaric than the grotesque practices of Islam."
2. He wants his reader to have a definite picture in mind of what Islamic punishment means; only then will he be able to compare it with Western punishment.
3. The public has the opportunity to *see* the punishment and to keep being reminded of it as it observes its victims walking about with scars and missing limbs. The author suggests that the reminder may well be more of a deterrent than forgetting a criminal once he is removed to his jail cell.
4. Prisoners are not rehabilitated in prison.
5. Conditions in our prisons are filled with horrible violence, overcrowding, and filth.
6. The absence of due process, the triviality of some of the crimes, the ritualistic mumbo jumbo in the pronouncements of Islamic law.
7. No, because he considers them barbaric even though they are really no more cruel than the punishments we mete out. What the author really wants us to do is to find a way to punish justly and without cruelty.

Answers to Questions About the Strategies

1. Paragraph 3: "Such traditions, we all must agree, are no sign of an advanced civilization. In the West. . . ."
2. He uses the following transitions: "First. . . . Then. . . . But the most distinctive element. . . ."
3. He is taking the opportunity to argue for prison reform in the West.
4. He uses block contrast, first describing at length Islamic punishment and then describing at length Western punishment.

5. He makes concessions when he needs to, but then he shows that despite the concessions, he is right. As an example, consider paragraph 17.

Answers to Questions About the Issues

1. It creates the problem of how to properly confine the perpetrators of heinous crimes and how to protect society from murder.
2. This question should promote a lively debate among your students. Allow for differing opinions.
3. Allow for individual suggestions.
4. Allow for individual opinions on these questions. The editors are in full agreement with Chapman's view that our penal system is in many ways cruel and barbaric. Often inmates become worse in prison than they were when they went in.
5. Allow for varying opinions. Since the editors believe in the innate dignity of man, they take the position that it is better to suffer the incorrigibility of a few than for the state to revert to the barbarism of capital punishment, which is irreversible and which gives the state a total lordship that belongs only to divinity.

George Orwell *A Hanging* (pp. 446-50)

Answers to Questions About the Facts

1. Perhaps Orwell is trying to say that anyone passively standing by while the life of another human being is forcibly destroyed is in a way responsible for "the unspeakable wrongness of cutting a life short when it is in full tide" (paragraph 10). Also, the combined role of observer and participant draws the reader into the action.
2. The advantage is that the reader can form judgments without accusing the author of preaching. The disadvantage is that the reporter must be careful to choose his details so that they inevitably lead the reader to the desired conclusion.
3. Orwell makes his purpose clear by his choice of details. The report is slanted because Orwell includes only those details that add to the horror of the hanging.
4. The dog does not discriminate against the man to be hanged; it even tries to lick the prisoner's face. After the execution the dog retreats into a corner of the yard as if ashamed of what has just taken place. Perhaps this is Orwell's way of saying that hangings are acts against nature (symbolized by the dog).
5. The prisoner's attempt to avoid the puddle is a testimony to man's ingrained desire to live. Intellectually the prisoner knows that he is

headed for death, but his natural instincts have not accepted the verdict. He acts as if he were going to live on.

6. Identity and guilt or innocence are irrelevant to this account. The point is that hanging itself, regardless of the reason, is wrong.

Answers to Questions About the Strategies

1. Orwell creates a gloomy, melancholy mood. Details:
   a. "sodden morning"
   b. "sickly light"
   c. "a row of sheds fronted with double bars, like small animal cages"
   d. "bare"
   e. "brown silent men"
   f. "condemned men"
2. The essay is filled with images and descriptions that add freshness. Example:
   Paragraph 2:   "It was like men handling a fish which is still alive and may jump back into the water. "
   Paragraph 11: "The gallows stood in a small yard, separate from the main grounds of the prison, and overgrown with tall prickly weeds."
   Paragraph 12: "It was a high, reiterated cry of 'Ram! Ram! Ram! Ram!' not urgent and fearful like a prayer or cry for help, but steady, rhythmical, almost like the tolling of a bell."
3. Paragraph 10: "It is curious, but till that moment I had never realized hat it means to destroy a healthy, conscious man."
   Paragraph 23: "I found that I was laughing quite loudly."
   The author singles himself out in order to emphasize his personal guilt in this hanging. If he feels guilty, perhaps the reader will feel guilty, too.
4. Orwell's method includes an appeal to the emotions and senses as well as to the intellect, whereas a strictly logical argument appeals to the reader's intellect only. Answers to this question will vary depending on whether your students are swayed by logic or by logic combined with emotion.

Answers to Questions About the Issues

1. Encourage students to be specific in their descriptions of the essay's effect on them. Did they feel sad? Indignant? Repelled? Indifferent?
2. A thoughtful reader will be struck by the fact that in the colonial environment described, the life of this Hindu prisoner was valued

no more highly than that of the dog trying to lick his face on the way to the gallows. For instance, the superintendent shows irritation when the arrangement for the hanging takes too long. He yells at the head jailer, "For God's sake hurry up, Francis. The man ought to have been dead by this time. Aren't you ready yet?"

3. Doubtless the tension of the hanging affected all of the bystanders, so that when the inevitable was over, relief was automatic. Perhaps, too, when one lives in a political atmosphere where death is meted out daily so that an individual life counts for little and death is common, one becomes inured to death and muffles one's agony. However, most readers are deeply saddened by this essay and claim that they would aggressively fight any government with such a tyrannical posture.

4. Allow for varying answers to this question.

5. Allow for individual answers. Since the essay is in reality an attempt to convince the reader of the "unspeakable wrongness of cutting a life short when it is in full tide," it should make no difference what manner of death is described. The central problem is the morality of capital punishment.

Chapter Eight ANALYZING: Comparison/Contrast, Division/Classification, and Causal Analysis

Ralph Waldo Emerson from *Conservatism and Liberalism* (pp. 457-59)

Answers to Questions About the Facts

1. Emerson means that human nature must have a primal commitment to the principles represented by conservatism and liberalism. Later he talks about these two forces existing and warring in nature.

2. Conservatism has the worst of the argument. Liberalism is sure of success because change is inevitable.

3. Conservatism holds to already established principle; hence, it is "all memory." The conservative values things for the way they are and draws his inspiration from the way things were. He is, therefore, very retrospective in his thinking.

4. Emerson lists these various weaknesses in paragraph 3. Among the weaknesses of conservatism are its distrust of nature, its lack of poetry, its opposition to change. The weaknesses of liberalism

include its egotism, its hypocrisy, its lack of prudence and husbandry.

5. He means that either one as a dominant trait in a person constitutes a defect. The complete man, according to Emerson, is one who has combined the best of conservatism and liberalism in his character.

Answers to Questions About the Strategies

1. The natural order of this sentence is inverted for effect.
2. This sentence is an example of parallelism. Another example: "Reform has no gratitude, no prudence, no husbandry."
3. This is a metaphor. *Castle* is a reference to the present state of values, which conservatism always sets out to defend.
4. A metaphor.
5. The use of the balanced sentence that pairs off contrasting elements without using a contrasting word or phrase. For example: "Conservatism is more candid to behold another's worth; reform more disposed to maintain and increase its own." Emerson uses the balanced sentence as the chief means of making contrasts in this essay.

Answers to Questions About the Issues

1. A number of issues could be cited. Here are some examples:
   Surrogate mothers: The liberals believe that surrogate mothers are a blessing for couples who can't have children; the conservatives consider the idea a malicious tampering with nature.
   Noncelibate priesthood: Liberal Catholics believe that married priests would be more successful since they would better understand family problems and would be sexually fulfilled. Conservative Catholics believe that a priest must be willing to be "married" to his calling and that, like Jesus, he will serve Christianity best if he does not have a family to dilute his devotion.
   Clothing styles: The liberals will wear the most trendy fashions, no matter how outrageous they appear, whereas the conservatives will tend to wear more traditional apparel.
   (For other issues, see the Issues sections at the ends of the text chapters.)
2. Allow for individual revelations and comments.
3. Allow for individual comments.
4. The editors have considerable admiration for the following persons, who seem to embody a well-balanced and moderate approach to life: Chief Justice Sandra O'Connor, writer M. Scott Peck (*The Road Less Travelled*), news commentator Hugh Downs.

Suzanne Britt *That Lean and Hungry Look* (pp. 461-63)

Answers to Questions About the Facts

1. She finds them too logical, compulsive, and efficient. She feels that they refuse to acknowledge life's essential mystery; consequently, they cannot give themselves to a *joie de vivre* and to the romance of spontaneity.

2. According to the author's research, any factor that makes a person unattractive may contribute to a kind of insecurity that leads to neurotic behavior. While it is true that many fat people indeed seem jolly, their jolliness can be a cover-up for feelings of rejection or inferiority. In our society, a slim person has a better chance of having a sense of self-worth than does a fat person. And as far as understanding the truth about life is concerned, that depends far more on a person's religious and philosophical background than on whether or not he or she is fat.

3. The list of three reasons why the author refuses to arrange all the parts of a jigsaw puzzle into groups according to size. The irony is that this list shows organization and logic, two characteristics appealing to the thin person.

4. The author has a two-fold serious purpose: First, she wants to gain your sympathy for fat people so that you don't judge them to be social outcasts but instead see them as attractive human beings. Second, she seems subtly to argue in favor of less emphasis on a scheduled, compulsively logical life and more emphasis on enjoying life's beauty and the pleasant intimacy of other people's company. She seems to be telling us that life is too short to spend all of our time seeking logical meanings or indulging in useful pursuits.

5. She claims that thin people are oppressive because they value the mind over the emotions. They prefer reasoned morality to happiness. For instance, they would rather discuss something as dull as a rutabaga vegetable than enjoy a fit of laughter.

Answers to Questions About the Strategies

1. The allusion originates from Shakespeare's *Julius Caesar*, where Caesar comments that Cassius has "that lean and hungry look" and therefore needs to be watched carefully. Another allusion appears in paragraph 9, where the author uses the phrase "acquainted with the night, " the title of a famous poem by Walt Whitman, describing a human being tortured by guilt and fear.

2.   The author uses the alternating method of contrasting fat and thin people; that is, she focuses on a basis for contrast, such as attitude toward fun, logic, and life's meaning and then she proceeds to alternate between thin people and fat people, showing how differently they react to these bases. The advantage of this method is the constant back-and-forth movement that makes the contrast immediate. Another method is the block method, where the author would first describe a thin person's view toward fun, logic, and life and then describe the fat person's view toward the same things. In this method, the contrast is not as immediate.

3.   The effect is a straightforward topic sentence that can be followed by details to prove its validity.

4.   Paragraph 4:   "They are crunchy *like carrots*" (a simile).

     Paragraph 5:   "The sides fat people see are *rounded blobs*" (metaphor).

     Paragraph 10: ". . . pat solutions loom *like dark clouds* (simile) over the *loose, comfortable, spread-out, soft world* (metaphor) of the fat."

     Other examples abound.

5.   First she uses vivid details. See, for instance, paragraph 10 for a vivid description of the contrast between bony, thin people and spread-out, fat people. Second, she either uses clichés as if they were brilliant new insights or she amends the cliché to say the opposite of its original meaning. See, for instance, paragraph 3—"If you clean it up today, it'll just get dirty again tomorrow. " Paragraph 4—"Thin people want to face the truth . Fat people know there is no truth. " Paragraph 5—"Fat people see all sides." Paragraph 6—"They know very well that God is not in his heaven and all is not right with the world." Paragraph 12—"They will cry in your beer with you. " Third, she uses a sarcastic and ironic tone, especially when dealing with thin people. See paragraph 2.

Answers to Questions About the Issues

1.   Emphasis on the slim, lean physique seems to have burgeoned along with the craze for jogging, walking, and aerobics. Americans are going through a phase of avid concern for the individual's health. We are warned against too much cholesterol, smoking, and heavy drinking. The image is one of athletic competence. Fat people do not fit this image.

2.   Leo suggests that today's slim-hipped look is a rebellion against male domination. See the editors' reasoning in the answer to question 1 above.

114

3. Obviously, Britt is not being logical in the strict sense of the word; however, this does not matter because her real point is that she would prefer being an instinctive, uninhibited, spontaneous person than a person who always tends to be logical, restrained, and worried. Britt uses the fat person as a symbol for a certain type of individual.
4. Encourage students to be imaginative. This exercise can be exceptionally humorous.
5. Whether or not appearance should influence success, the fact is that it does. Sometimes the influence is ironic. For instance, employees working behind the cameras in a T.V. studio are expected to dress in jeans and sweat shirts, to give an extremely casual (if not sloppy) appearance. In that setting, the person wearing a suit and tie or a lovely silk dress would seem ridiculous. On the other hand, bankers and lawyers are expected to wear conservative but dressy clothes. Recently, numerous articles and books have been written on the subject of dressing for success.

Gilbert Highet *Diogenes and Alexander* (pp. 465-69)

Answers to Questions About the Facts

1. They share knowledge, honesty, insight, talent, intellectual curiosity, the power to influence, and fame.
2. Diogenes is poor; Alexander is wealthy. Diogenes conquered men intellectually; Alexander conquered nations physically. Diogenes's lifestyle is simple and uncluttered, so that he deals only with the essentials of life; Alexander's lifestyle is complicated and elaborate. Diogenes is often ridiculed; Alexander is revered. Diogenes is experienced; Alexander is not.
3. He wanted to fit into the scheme of nature and exist like other animals, without man-created artificiality. For him, elaborate living brought worries and misery. Discuss the difference between his motivation and that of Thoreau, who wanted to confront life at its core in order to judge whether or not it was good.
4. Possessions and complex living produce worries and drain one of energy. The rich man gives up personal freedom in order to take care of his riches.
5. Diogenes was practical and democratic, whereas Plato and Aristotle were theoretical and elitist. Plato and Aristotle used formal classrooms for teaching, whereas Diogenes taught outside in the crowded areas of Corinth.
6. Alexander is not hot-tempered about Diogenes's seeming lack of courtesy. Also, his statement, "If I were not Alexander, I should be

Diogenes," indicates that, unlike the ordinary observer, he understood Diogenes's outlook on life.

7. Cynicism was a doctrine founded on the idea that all men are motivated by selfishness, and that consequently self-control is the highest virtue to be sought. As one of the world's most brilliant warriors and a leader of men, Alexander must have had ample opportunity to confirm this doctrine.

Answers to Questions About the Strategies

1. Paragraph 11.
2. Highet draws separate portraits. Since Diogenes is described first, the reader will use him as a kind of measuring stick by which to judge Alexander when he is described. This method also requires that the reader use his own imagination to draw conclusions about who is superior, Diogenes or Alexander.
3. Varying interpretations: (a) If I were not Alexander, I would want to be Diogenes. (b) If it were not for the fact that I am Alexander, I would be in the same circumstances as Diogenes.
4. "Sometimes they threw jeers, and got jibes; . . . "
5. It is a figure of speech or a metaphor. It means "to take the clean metal of human life, to erase the old false conventional markings, and to imprint it with its true values" (paragraph 5).
6. "He thought most people were only half-alive, most men only half-men. " It is developed by examples.

Answers to Questions About the Issues

1. The students' answers will depend on whether they consider power more important than personal freedom. Alexander, conqueror of the world, had power; Diogenes, the ruggedly independent philosopher, had personal freedom.
2. The connection is clearly between the owner of the wood and Alexander, because both are burdened with the responsibility of material things that must be organized, supervised, kept safe, and retained. The time demanded by such responsibility robs the owner of time to be creative, and he must always worry that some power sooner or later will step in to rob him of his possessions.
3. Allow for open discussion on this point. Encourage students to be specific. For instance, ask them how they would feel if they had no privacy and all natural acts were performed in public.
4. The editors consider the subjects, even poetry, highly important. Philosophy still attempts to answer the basic questions of life; poetry provides a vehicle for understanding the depths of human

116

joys and sorrows; scientific investigation helps to expand knowledge in all areas. We would add history, which attempts to maintain a perspective on life, and perhaps other fine arts, such as painting and music, which attempt to beautify one's existence.

5.   Allow for individual responses to these questions.

Bruce Catton *Grant and Lee: A Study in Contrasts* (pp. 471-74)

Answers to Questions About the Facts

1.   Answered in paragraph 5. Lee represented tidewater Virginia and the Southern aristocracy.
2.   Grant represented the ideal of the rugged Westerner. He was the son of a tanner on the western frontier.
3.   Grant was future-oriented. He believed in democracy because he had grown up under it.
4.   Answered in paragraphs 10 and 11. Lee was committed to the idea of a regional static society, while Grant was equally committed to a broader concept of society. That is the most striking contrast between them.
5.   Because at Appomattox both men showed an ability to turn quickly to peace.

Answers to Questions About the Strategies

1.   It is somewhat arbitrary whether to begin the contrast with Grant or with Lee. However, since Lee represented the defeated as well as the lost ideal, there is an element of logic in sketching his characteristics first.
2.   This is a transitional paragraph leading into the portrait of Lee. Moreover, it is an important general idea which the next paragraph will amplify.
3.   "On the other hand. "
4.   The author is not simply discussing each man as himself but as examples of two opposing types that fought the Civil War. The discussion of the type represented by each man is therefore important to the overall discussion.
5.   This paragraph functions to juxtapose the two men, not merely as opposing generals but as opposing American types. Paragraphs that follow amplify this discussion.

Answers to Questions About the Issues

1. Certainly the importance of family and culture still survives among many members of the wealthy class—especially in the East and South. The power of a landed nobility, of course, has given way to ownership of huge corporations. But these corporations are often owned by a family (the Fords, the Rockefellers, the Mellons, the Carnegies), who still have a strong sense of obligation to their country, as revealed in their generous financial support of scientific research, of museum expansion, of music and dance, and of excellence in literature. Without them, our cultural heritage would have been placed in jeopardy.

2. Allow for open discussion or debate on this subject. The editors believe that poverty and slavery are best combatted by the frontier spirit. Yet, where the aristocratic spirit has been crushed altogether, beauty and the arts disappear. Consider the Soviet Union and China, where revolution has outlawed the aristocracy, to the point of elimination of much great art and high culture.

3. Allow for varying views on these questions. You might use the following subjects as focal points of the discussion: the marriage ceremony, including a bride with a white gown and veil; the graduation ceremony, including academic regalia; Thanksgiving dinner, including turkey and pumpkin pie.

4. Queen Victoria, who could trace her lineage back to a long line of English, Belgian, and German kings, and who wore the crown of imperial Britain—contrasted with Mary Todd Lincoln, who came from a good upper-middle-class family in Kentucky and became wife of President Lincoln, known for his representation of the common man in a democratic nation.

5. Allow for individual opinions on this question. President Theodore Roosevelt (1858-1919) was an ardent supporter of expansion.

O. Henry, *Proof of the Pudding* (p.475-83)

Answers to Questions About the Facts

1. Westbrook rejects Dawe's stories because he is convinced that at the dramatic climax of these stories Dawe lapses into ordinary instead of elevated language.

2. Whereas Westbrook insists that in times of crisis the characters in fiction must reflect the dramatic moment by using dramatic and high-flown speeches, Dawe believes that the opposite is true because in real life the more distressed a person is, the less he or she is able to express that distress in heroic language and will lapse

118

into halting, inept, fumbling phrases used under ordinary circumstances. Modern fiction leans in the direction of Dawe, attempting to reflect in fiction the language of ordinary human intercourse.

3.   From deep and powerful emotions.

4.   He means that when a human being confronts tragedy in real life, he will not utter trite, banal words, but words of high tragedy. To "mirror" life means to reflect what actually happens in life.

5.   He agrees because he is sure that the experiment will prove him right. He is going to enjoy this experiment the way a vivisectionist enjoys cutting up animals.

Answers to Questions About the Strategies

1.   These paragraphs tell us that the story is written from the point of view of an omniscient narrator, who thinks nothing of intruding into his own narrative to address his readers personally. This technique can be humorous or serious, but whether humorous or serious, it keeps the reader conscious of the fact that the narrator is the one in charge of the plots and characters.

2.   Westbrook is portrayed as pompously knowledgeable whereas Dawe is portrayed as dingy and somewhat ragged (see paragraphs 5 and 6) Westbrook is called "Editor Westbrook" whereas Dawe is referred to by his ridiculous name, "Shackleford Dawe" or "Shack" for short. The former is drawn as a respected literary figure, the latter as a writer manqué.

3.   He prepares us by telling us that Dawe plans a real-life test to find out whether people in overwhelming circumstances use high-flown language or ordinary language. Actually, the narrator does not convince us because he develops a surprise reversal at the end of the story for which we are not prepared.

4.   He manages to create vivid characters whose dialogue clearly reveals their personalities. He also loves to surprise his readers with ironic reversals at the end of his stories. For instance, in his famous Christmas story, "The Gift of the Magi," a wife sells her beautiful hair to buy her husband a gold chain for his watch while the husband sells his beautiful watch to buy combs for his wife's hair. In the story you have just read, the trick the men plan to play on Dawe's wife backfires when both wives leave their husbands and take off to join the chorus of an opera company. But the ultimate surprise lies in the language used as the two men react to the wives' departure. Dawe uses highly dramatic language whereas Westbrook stutters illiterate phrases.

Answers to Questions About the Issues

1. As the story proves, under pressure people will reveal various kinds of linguistic styles. Some will wax poetic whereas others will stutter and mutter. Some will remain in control whereas others will fall apart.
2. Many artists remain poor and ignored because they are innovators who break with tradition to create a new literary style. Often editors or critics cannot adjust to new artistic waves. But a genuine artist will never sell out for the comfort of having money. No, some artistic geniuses have died in complete destitution. (e.g. the poet Keats, the painter van Gogh, the writer Edgar Allan Poe).
3. Dawe will have to admit that under stress some people can use dramatic language. Westbrook will have to admit that under stress some people stammer and stutter.
4. This is a question that will elicit moral views on marriage relationships. Students should feel free to state how they feel about the two wives. Was Louise right in running away from a starving writer? Was Mrs. Westbrook right in running away from an unfeeling and boring husband?

Alastair Reid *Curiosity* (pp. 485-86)

Answers to Questions About the Facts

1. It is really a poem about two kinds of people--those who take risks and those who don't.
2. Advantages: One remains dynamic; one is not naively gullible; one investigates the truth; one leads the only kind of life worth living.

   Disadvantages: One lives in danger; one is accused of being irresponsible; one may lose one's life.
3. Dogs are threatened by the untraditional and unpredictable ways of cats. Dogs love security and convention.
4. Cats, because they experience life.

Answers to Questions About the Strategies

1. The poet feels that each day one lives, one is also in the process of dying. He also implies that anyone who lives without curiosity or without taking risks is "dead" even though he or she may be biologically alive.

2. The poem is emphasizing that people who search for the simple but perfect life (the idyllic life) will in the process most likely experience a great deal of pain (hell).
3. They symbolize people who lead conventional, ordinary, trite lives and who have no ideas of their own.
4. A person who has repeatedly faced terrible dangers or risks but who has been lucky enough to survive. The saying goes that cats have nine lives; that is why they never get killed even though they fall off roofs, are chased by other animals, or are fed poison.
5. The pursuit of a full life and the pursuit of true love both take daring.

Answers to Questions About the Issues

1. Allow for differing personal preferences. Probably those students who dislike taking risks and being experimental will prefer dogs, whereas those who look for new horizons, new ways of dealing with the present, and new adventures will love cats.
2. Have students suggest their own candidates for dogdom or catdom. The editors suggest that people like Stanley and Livingston, the American pilgrims, Madame Curie, Martin Luther, and Albert Einstein were extreme cats. People like Louis XVII of France, Pope Leo X (who opposed Luther's reforms), the loyalists of New England (in 1776), and members of the Spanish Inquisition were extreme dogs. In between the two extremes lie the great majority of thinkers and doers.
3. The poem is slanted in favor of cats. Whereas dogs are made to look dull, tedious, and unimaginative in their determination to preserve the predictable and decent status quo, cats are made to look exciting, dashing, and imaginative in their quest for the deeper meanings of life.
4. Allow for individual tastes in choosing one kind over another.
5. The editors propose that in an ideal society, the dogs should outnumber the cats; otherwise society is doomed to chaos without rules or order. While cats are a necessity for any society wishing to make progress through intuitive discoveries and daring experiments, dogs are nonetheless the bedrock of society in that they cherish traditions, the proven good, and responsible behavior. Cats are liberal, reaching into the future; dogs are conservative, clinging to the past. In sum, a thriving environment requires both "cats" and "dogs," but perhaps more "dogs" than "cats."

William Golding *Thinking as a Hobby* (pp. 489-95)

Answers to Questions About the Facts

1. The types of thinking are:

   Grade-three: prejudice, hypocrisy
   Grade-two: discovering prejudice and hypocrisy
   Grade-one: doing something to change prejudice and hypocrisy

   The very word *grade* implies a value judgment. The rarest and highest grade is one—only a few creative, courageous people reach that level.

2. Golding takes time to describe his teachers because they were supposed to teach their students how to become profound thinkers; yet most of these teachers had never gone beyond grade-three thinking. Here is a loaded question for your students: How do you rate the thinking level of most of your teachers?

3. Grade-one thinking requires that one step over people's conventions and prejudices. This may be unpopular and cause one to be lonely, isolated, alienated. Your class will profit from a discussion of which politicians, educators, or scientists today come closest to being grade-one thinkers.

4. One can assume that the author is more devoted than ever to grade-one thinking, since he tells us that he has become professional rather than remaining an amateur thinker. But he also leaves the reader with the impression that grade-one thinking is dangerous because man's animal nature is always ready to pounce on and destroy the true thinker.

5. That communication is important to any kind of thinking.

Answers to Questions About the Strategies

1. The statuettes are explained in paragraph 3. The explanation is necessary because not all readers would have recognized the statues and their meanings.

2. The boy interprets the statues with a child's imagination. For example, he sees the Venus de Milo as in a panic lest her towel slip down and expose her nakedness. He sees the leopard as springing down at the top drawer of the filing cabinet. He sees the thinker as utterly miserable. Golding brings out the boy's accurate intuitive awareness of his teacher's hypocrisies. Golding describes a child's typical fear of school authorities (see paragraph 4).

3. The neck is a symbol for hypocrisy; that is, a person can point in one direction while his neck strains in another.
4. Grade-three thinkers are compared with a herd of cows grazing on a hill, all facing the same direction on the hillside. It is an appropriate analogy because it connotes lack of thought, following the herd.
5. Jailing Nehru and Gandhi was an act of prejudice; not joining the League of Nations was an act of hypocrisy.

Answers to Questions About the Issues

1. Grade-one thinking can take place in any area of human endeavor. Galileo focused on astronomy, Edison on electricity, Luther on religion. The main requirement is that the grade-one thinker be willing to reason independently and to create something original—and this, indeed, may mean replacing an old system.
2. Encourage students to remember anecdotes from elementary school-punishments, maxims, attitudes shown by their teachers.
3. The conformist, because he gains his sense of identity by joining a group and being like the others in the group.
4. The importance of grade-two thinking lies in its ability to detect situations that do not make sense, either because they are contradictory or because they are absurd. Because grade-two thinking is iconoclastic and challenges the status quo, it is an important step toward grade-one thinking. One must wipe out nonsense or evil before replacing it with something better.
5. Nature gets in the way. Humans have strong natural urges, such as the urge for sex, for food, and for shelter. These urges often displace a person's grade-one aspirations. One need only consider the many artists, politicians, or clergymen who aspired to creative monuments that would have improved society, but failed in their aspirations because nature got in the way in the form of a lover, chemical abuse, or a craving for money. Have your students suggest the names of individuals who are known for what they might have accomplished.

John Holt *Kinds of Discipline* (pp. 497-500)

Answers to Questions About the Facts

1. He divides discipline according to three sources: Nature, society, and superior force.
2. He uses five examples: (a) a child building a tower out of blocks; (b) a child playing the piano; (c) a child driving a nail; (d) a child

building something; (e) a child playing baseball. The examples are common and so will be recognized readily by all readers.
3. The learner gets instant feedback; the feedback is clear and often points toward how and why to correct one's error; the feedback is unbiased.
4. Allow for open discussion.
5. "When it is necessary to protect the life, health, safety, or well-being of people or other living creatures, or to prevent destruction of things that people care about" (paragraph 3).
6. The desire to want to do a given thing well.

Answers to Questions About the Strategies

1. He is personifying nature as a woman--who is objective and has integrity.
2. "The first and most important" (paragraph 1). "The next discipline" (paragraph 2). "The third discipline" (paragraph 3). "There are places where all three disciplines overlap" (paragraph 4). These guideposts help the reader to keep track of Holt's three-part division and of his final paragraph, where he indicates that the three kinds of disciplines overlap in certain places.
3. This allusion is satirical; it suggests a kind of bantam rooster—a man who gains stature by bullying others.

Answers to Questions About the Issues

1. Various answers are possible: table manners, holding back tears when hurt (especially boys), good sportsmanship in children's games, etc.
2. Allow for various suggestions. In the past, these answers have been proposed: Always study at a preplanned time and in a place used only for study. Begin to study the moment you sit down to do so; do not daydream in order to escape studying. If you are studying a textbook, underline and make marginal notes. Pick an environment that suits your personality—some people concentrate best when engulfed by music or other noises; others can concentrate only in absolute silence.
3. In our society the result would doubtless be a social misfit because the child would grow up never having adopted the limitations set by society.
4. Ultimately, the abuser must rely on all three kinds of discipline, especially the discipline of a superior force—either spiritual or imposed by an enormous act of self will.
5. Allow for individual answers.

Francis Bacon *The Idols* (pp. 502-03)

Answers to Questions About the Facts

1. Obstructions to the search for truth are being divided. In Bacon's day, the word *idol* meant something visible but without substance. Thus an idol worshiper would be a person who worships blindly.
2. All the idols are false notions deeply rooted in human thought.
   a. Idols of the tribe are false notions that result from the inaccuracy of the human senses.
   b. Idols of the den are false notions that result from man's environment—his family, his education, his church, and so forth. In short, they are the bases of prejudice.
   c. Idols of the market are false notions that result from semantic confusion.
   d. Idols of the theater are false notions that result from systems constructed by philosophers or scientists.
3. Bacon believes that the only way humankind can rid itself of these idols is to be warned against them and to be on guard. In other words, people must become aware of these false notions and then they must fight against their influence. He suggests that true induction (careful observation of evidence) is the best remedy.

Answers to Questions About the Strategies

1. Bacon's thought is logical and precise; and so is his style.
2. Archaic words: *instauration* (paragraph 1), *confutation* (paragraph 3), *denominate* (paragraph 7). Archaic phrases (ones that are characteristically roundabout); "uneven mirrors, which impart their own properties to different objects" (uneven mirrors that reflect unevenly)(paragraph 4); "at the will of the generality" (by general consent)(paragraph 6); "perverted rules of demonstration" (wrong rules used to prove a point) (paragraph 7).
3. Bacon uses induction to prove his point; that is, he carefully observes and lists the false notions that have influenced society in its search for truth (see answer to content question 2). Then Bacon concludes that the only way to avoid these errors in the future is to identify them and guard against them.
4. Bacon uses the analogy of the theater. He compares philosophic and scientific systems to theater productions. The analogy helps to clarify Bacon's views that these systems are figments of the imagination, creating fictitious worlds, just as a play creates a fictitious world.

Answers to Questions About the Issues

1. See Alan Simpson's "Marks of an Educated Man" (pp. 202-07) and William Golding's "Thinking as a Hobby" (pp. 489-95. Notice that much of what these two contemporary writers say about the process of thinking is similar to Bacon's views, especially their ideas about prejudice and lack of enlightenment.
2. Since "idols of the tribe" are obstructions resulting from the inaccuracy of the human senses, one can cite numerous examples: vanishing lines that appear to make parallel train tracks converge in the distance; mistaking a roll of thunder for an earthquake; confusing a piece of crystal with ice.
3. Have students read Orwell's "Politics of the English Language" (pp. 611-22). The study of semantics indicates that wars can break out between countries when one society does not understand another society's interpretation of important terms, such as "defense," "authority," "self determination," "sovereignty," "human rights," and so forth.
4. Encourage students to share certain moral, political, or social ideas they received from either their parents, their school, or their church.
5. The idea, promoted by many T.V. evangelists, that spiritual perfection can be bought with money; the idea that taking drugs can elevate one's consciousness; the idea that scholarship can be achieved through painless shortcuts; the idea that making money is more important than enhancing one's character, and so forth. Encourage students to add to the list.

Bart Edelman, *English 101* (pp. 505-06)

Answers to Questions About the Facts

1. The action takes place in a college classroom, as indicated by the title of the poem (English 101 is the name commonly listed in college catalogs for freshman composition).
2. People who are "astray" are wandering about like cattle in a herd, seemingly not sure of their path. Freshman Composition is often the first class students must take in college. Thus, it can be said that they wander into class as part of a herd of students, astray—not sure of where they are headed, destined to succeed or to fail.
3. The figure of speech is called a metonymy, in which the poet uses a part of something to represent the whole. In other words, the

126

word "brain" is used to represent the head, allowing for a double meaning to the sentence "He drops his brain / Upon the desk. . . ." It could mean that the boy simply places his head on the desk to rest, or it could also mean that he refuses to think.

4. One student speaks up just as the bell rings to indicate the close of the class hour.

Answers to Questions About Strategies

1. Students are classified into three types: the uninterested, the compulsive, and the true scholar.
2. He wants to stress the importance of a student so fascinated by the subject being discussed that he raises his "hand" to speak (using his "voice") even though class time has run out.
3. English 101 is probably the most universal and basic course in college, and most students see it simply as a tedious prerequisite to the advanced courses more suited to the students' specialized interests, such as advanced mathematics or economics.
4. He is comparing the intellectual dialogue between teacher and student to sifting through grains of wheat—at last coming up with ideas for writing a composition.

Answers to Questions About the Issues

1. Various wordings would be acceptable answers, but the sentence would say something like, "Many different types of students take English 101 or Freshman Composition, with widely differing results."
2. The greatest challenge is to capture the students interest and set them to thinking about ideas—wondering, questioning—and eventually writing about these ideas.
3. Neither student is ideal, but the girl of stanza 3 is at least willing to work whereas the boy of stanza 2 must somehow be awakened and captivated by learning. If the teacher can challenge the girl to think on her own, she will make a fine student whereas the boy will need to develop the skills of concentration and diligence. Allow students to speculate on the academic future of both kinds of students.
4. Allow for open debate on this question. The subject should lead into a discussion of present-day students' writing skills. Can freshman composition improve one's writing skills? How? Consider such matters as the instructor's critiques, discussing fertile ideas, and practice in setting thoughts on paper.
5. Freshman composition courses typically involve a certain body of reading from an anthology of well-known material, among which

Frost's poem "The Road Not Taken" and Mark Twain's novel *Huck-leberry Finn* are often required reading. Have students discuss these works and their influence. You might have them compare "The Road Not Taken" with "Design" (p. 535).

Roger Rosenblatt *Why the Justice System Fails* (pp. 510-14)

Answers to Questions About the Facts

1. *Thesis,* as stated in the final sentence of the first paragraph: "It is not that there are no mechanisms in place to deal with American crime, merely that the existing ones are impractical, inefficient, anachronistic, uncooperative, and often lead to as much civic destruction as they are meant to curtail." *Key words:* "impractical," "inefficient," "anachronistic," "uncooperative," "civic destruction."
2. Rosenblatt cites seven causes:
   1. There is a lack of effective cooperation between the police and the prosecutors.
   2. The majority of criminals go free.
   3. Plea bargaining debases the system.
   4. Trial delays clog the courts.
   5. Easy bail results in serious crimes.
   6. The lack of prison space results in early release from prison or in not taking in prisoners.
   7. Juvenile crime is not properly handled. Allow for open discussion on the last question.
3. Every citizen has the right to a speedy trial. A speedy trial is fair for the victim as well as for the alleged criminal. When long segments of time elapse between the perpetration of a crime and its resolution in court, justice is almost impossible because time will have covered too many tracks and the facts of the case will be blurred.
4. The matter is difficult because in our system of justice a person is innocent until proven guilty. Thus, unless it can be established beyond doubt that a suspect is likely to jump bail or to commit a violent act when he is out on bail, the suspect must be given the benefit of the doubt.
5. The police accuse the judges of being lazy; the judges accuse the police of neglecting to bring in the evidence. Further evidence exists to indicate that the courts are simply overloaded and therefore cannot operate efficiently.
6. Rosenblatt doubtless means that in any future reform, the judges will err on the side of leniency and mercy toward the accused because they do not want to regress to a medieval atmosphere of tyranny or arbitrary rule.

Answers to Questions About the Strategies

1. Paragraphs 2 and 3 offer convincing statistics to indicate that one problem inherent in the system of justice is that a huge number of criminals never get apprehended.

2. The subject developed is *trial delays*. The reasons for devoting four paragraphs to this subject is to demonstrate how different forms of trial delays erect barriers to speedy justice.

3. In each case the quotation adds expert testimony to Rosenblatt's contentions. He is careful to quote people of knowledge and influence, such as the New York Police Commissioner (paragraph 3); the Detroit Deputy Police Chief (paragraph 7); George Deukmejian, who became Governor of California (paragraph 8); the Executive Director of the Chicago Crime Commission (paragraph 12); criminal-court justice Lois Forer (paragraph 12).

4. They are all references to terms that liberalize the law and consequently reflect a permissive attitude toward the criminal.

5. All of these expressions can be understood through their contexts:
   a. Plea bargaining means reducing the charge by having the criminal admit to a lesser charge.
   b. Copping a plea means having the defendant plead guilty to a lesser charge.
   c. Continuances are trials that are postponed.
   d. Dispositions are trials that have been completed.
   e. Procedural delays are delays due to some procedural technicality.
   f. Pretrial means anything that happens before the trial.

Answers to Questions About the Issues

1. Allow for open discussion on this question. One prevailing opinion is that too many criminals are never apprehended because society is indifferent. No one wants to get involved in pursuing a suspected criminal.

2. Allow students to express individual opinions. Doubtless the conservative student will express a wish for stricter courts whereas the more liberal student will warn that excessive strictness can lead to a totalitarian system in which no justice, only tyrannic cruelty, prevails.

3. Allow freedom of opinion on all of the questions posed. One trend is evident: psychologists specializing in adolescent crime no longer romanticize young boys or girls who are chronic criminals. Rather, they view them as being in need of intense therapy, which may or

may not cure them. As a whole, society has become more cynical about the problems of youthful crime.
4. Allow for varying opinions on this problem. The class might consider the idea of finding better ways to reduce crime—through stronger family ties, quality education, reduced poverty, building better self-images in young people, and lessening the stress of surviving in our complex society.
5. Have students come up with two or three good reasons why plea bargaining must remain a possibility.

George Gilder *Why Men Marry* (pp. 516-19)

Answers to Questions About the Facts

1. The young man seems to be giving up his freedom to chase all of the exciting pursuits connected with sex, as mentioned in paragraph 1.
2. The urge for immortality provided by children.
3. *Alchemy* means "a magical power to transform. " Neither scientists nor scholars fully understand how love can transform a man from a bitter and disillusioned being into a tender husband and father, but they have seen the results.
4. It is the ominous premonition that youth is waning, time is running out, and death is lurking somewhere, ready to claim the man.
5. The energies that form the basis of a civilized society.

Answers to Questions About the Strategies

1. By asking the titillating question, What does a man get out of marriage that he does not get simply by having sex with women? This question is certainly of universal interest.
2. It connotes a "macho" male taking off at high speed in his sports car to seek some high adventure because he is not tied down to a home and wife.
3. Through the parallelism of repeating *in the* ("in the womb . . . in the world. . . . In the swelter . . . in the shape . . . in the protective support. . .")
4. The effect is perhaps shocking. Doubtless the author used this word to debase the sex act as performed by the disillusioned bachelor.
5. A trap, which is an apt metaphor to show how the carefree, freedom loving bachelor suddenly feels life closing in on him. For other metaphors, see paragraph 14: "in the grips of it" (personification),

"fires and storms" (metaphors), "burn his signature into the covenant of a specific life" (symbol).

Answers to Questions About the Issues

1. Men marry because by falling in love and having children they achieve a form of immortality.
2. Allow for individual advice. One suggestion is not to marry too young. When a couple marry in their teens, one or the other may feel cheated out of the fun and excitement of dating and experiencing various kinds of encounters with persons of the opposite sex.
3. It has been suggested by confirmed bachelors that certain careers (art, the priesthood) are so demanding that a married man cannot devote himself properly to his work. Some bachelors claim that they avoid great tedium by remaining free of domesticity.
4. Allow for a free discussion on this topic. Divorce statistics indicate that our system of marrying for love is not successful. Perhaps we need to heighten our awareness about what makes successful marriages. Young people need better training in being good mates and in selecting mates who will complement their lives.
5. The author takes the view, held by many, that women ennoble men and that the baser side of man is elevated when he falls in love. Doubtless some students will disagree with this view.

Henry David Thoreau *Why I Went to the Woods* (pp. 521-26)

Answers to Questions About the Facts

1. He says in the first paragraph, "I went to the woods because I wished to live deliberately, to front only the essential facts of life, and see if I could not learn what it had to teach, and not, when I came to die, discover that I had not lived." Thoreau thinks that the nation fritters its life away with detail. He is against the pettiness of commerce and regulation.
2. He means that we are consumed by the engines of our commerce. In other words, our lives are wasted away in the petty transactions of business and trivia.
3. In paragraph 4 Thoreau writes, "If you are acquainted with the principle, what do you care for a myriad instances and applications?" This idea of a new *principle* is behind Thoreau's implied definition of "news." To be news, the event must involve a new principle. If the principle is old, then the report of the event is not news, but "gossip."

4. Thoreau is playing with the idea of what psychologists call a "perceptual set": we see in the world what our frame of mind predisposes us to see. He says that if we have our minds filled with trivia and pettiness, the entire world will conform to this picture. It will seem filled with petty detail, with shams and appearances.

5. Truth is to be found in the here and now (paragraph 6). Thoreau says that truth is not remote, nor is it to be found in the "outskirts of the system, behind the farthest star, before Adam and after the last man." Rather, all "times and places and occasions are now and here. " We are prevented from finding truth because our minds are clogged with trivia and pettiness.

Answers to Questions About the Strategies

1. He is being ironic.

2. These anecdotes have in common an Eastern origin. They indicate that Thoreau was heavily involved in Eastern religious thought. The anecdotes also add an exotic flavor to his writing.

3. This figure is a metaphor. Thoreau writes in a highly metaphoric style; examples are to be found throughout the article. In paragraph 1, for instance: "I wanted to live deep and suck out all the marrow of life, to live so sturdily and Spartanlike as to put to rout all that was not life, to cut a broad swath and shave close, to drive life into a corner, and reduce it to its lowest terms, and, if it proved to be mean, well then to get the whole genuine meanness of it, and publish its meanness to the world; or if it were sublime, to know it by experience, and be able to give a true account of it in my next excursion. " Thoreau frequently piles metaphor upon metaphor, as in this example. His heavy use of metaphors accounts for the vivid and colorful effect of his prose style.

4. This is a simile, distinguished from the metaphor by its use of "like" to introduce the compared terms.

5. The allusion in paragraph 7 is to Ulysses tied to the mast. This episode is found in the *Odyssey*. Allusions are useful because they can shorten tedious explanation if the appropriate event can be pointed out. However, they add a complex flavor to a writer's style by assuming that the reader is familiar with the same literary work. Allusions work well in prose written for people with the same background as the author. However, they do not work well if the author is attempting to communicate something to an audience whose literary background is different from his or her own.

Answers to Questions About the Issues

1. They both insist that people should simplify their lives. Allow for open discussion on the last two questions.
2. Television is seen by many as a monster that controls the lives of citizens who are mesmerized by it, to the point where they neglect important duties.
3. Allow for individual views on this subject. One side of the argument is that our mailboxes today are littered with catalogs, public information materials, advertisements, and political views; the other side is that the post office has made it convenient for us to pay our bills and to correspond with people who live at great distances from us.
4. Thoreau found that he needed modest amounts of food, exercise, and shelter for survival. He found that thinking profound thoughts was one of the essential elements of his existence.
5. Allow students to share their experiences with the class.

Kate Chopin *The Storm* (pp. 528-33)

Answers to Questions About the Facts

1. Obviously they were passionate lovers at one time, as inferred from the reference to Assumption, where Alcee had kissed Calixta so passionately that in order to save her virginity, he took flight. For reasons not revealed in the story, both lovers married someone else.
2. The violent storm seems to evoke the violent passions lying dormant in Alcée and Calixta. The storm is an excuse for sheltering Alcée and it also provides a safe period of time when the lovers can be alone because Bobinôt will not be able to walk home with Bibi; he will need to remain sheltered until the storm abates.
3. Paragraphs 24 and 25 imply that the lovers had not found fulfillment for their erotic desires until this moment. They seem to have solid marriages that lack sexual passion. Allow for open discussion on the second question.
4. They act as if it had never taken place. Calixta welcomes her husband and four-year-old son; then the family enjoys a relaxed and laughter filled dinner. Alcée writes an affectionate letter to his wife and she answers in similar fashion. Have students discuss the plausibility of the reactions.
5. Later, in paragraph 24, we know that the lovers are in the bedroom because they are described as lying in "that dim, mysterious" chamber. Thus the description serves as a foreshadowing of events.

Answers to Questions About the Strategies

1. The setting is a Creole community in Louisiana, where they speak a French *patois*. The setting adds regional color and may even make the passionate encounter more believable.
2. With each new Roman numeral a shift in setting takes place. In I, the focus is on Bobinôt and Bibi; in II, the focus shifts to Calixta; in III, back to Bobinôt and Bibi; in IV to Alcée; and in V, to Alcée's wife, Clarisse. The Roman numerals help the reader make the shift without confusion.
3. She resorts to figures of speech.
   Paragraph 24: "She was a revelation (metaphor) . . . like a creamy lily" (simile).
   Paragraph 25: "The generous abundance of her passion . . . was like a white flame" (simile).
4. The title is appropriate to the content of the story because two storms take place—the storm of the natural physical world and the passionate storm inside the two lovers. Also, just as nature's storms are followed by quiet so the storm of passion is followed by a peaceful family life.
5. The climax takes place when the conflict between whether to make love or not make love is resolved and the lovers give in to their passion. The rest of the story is mere denouement, untying the knots and getting the characters back to normal.

Answers to Questions About the Issues

1. This discussion may lead to strong disagreement among your students. The key part of the question, however, is the fact that they did yield. Now, how are they to proceed with their lives, given the circumstances? Certainly, to break up two families because of a brief and impulsive love affair during a storm seems unwarranted. Moreover, to confess to their mates what the lovers have done would only cause bitterness and sorrow, so why do it? We believe that the lovers did the only acceptable thing. Whether or not they should have yielded in the first place is an entirely different moral question.
2. Apparently, Calixta's husband has not evoked from her the same passionately sensual response that Alcée did. A chemistry exists between Calixta and Alcée that neither has been able to create with another person. The lovers are overwhelmed by this sexual attraction. Of Alcée it is said that "The generous abundance of her passion, without guile or trickery, was like a white flame which

134

penetrated and found response in depths of his own sensuous nature that had never yet been reached."

3. No doubt they were shocked by its permissiveness—describing a woman who betrays her husband on an impulse. Allow students to voice their own opinions about the characters in the story.

4. They seem to lead a pleasantly conventional family life, focused on the children. The husbands seem to cater to their wives, with Bobinôt bringing Calixta some shrimp and with Alcée allowing Clarisse to extend her vacation.

5. Human passions can be powerful and may, for the moment, overcome rational behavior.

Robert Frost *Design* (pp. 535)

Answers to Questions About the Facts

1. They are accidents of nature since they all deviate from their normal colors (black for the spider, blue for the heal-all, brown for the moth) and are unexpectedly white. Also, by accident (or by chance), they converge in the same place. Ironically, although they are the color of purity and innocence, the poet labels them "assorted characters of death and blight." We can thus infer that these characters have no active say in either their natures or their actions.

2. Is there some divine intelligence guiding the various situations and actions on this earth? If there is such an intelligence, it cannot be clearly discerned and its direction is horrifying.

3. His argument goes something like this: If there is any design at all in such an insignificant detail as the meeting of the spider, the heal-all, and the moth, then the design is not only sinister but also horrifying because the spider has killed the moth while the heal-all stands by helplessly.

4. God is a *sufficient* cause.

Answers to Questions About the Strategies

1. Four similes: "Like a white piece of rigid satin cloth," "Like the ingredients of a witches' broth," "like a froth," and "like a paper kite." One metaphor: "snow-drop spider." Allow for individual responses concerning the effect of each example.

2. *Kindred* means having the same origin, nature, or character. The poet is stressing the First Cause that created both the spider and the heal-all.

3. *Brought, steered, govern.*

Answers to Questions About the Issues

1. Most of us wonder about who is in charge of the universe when our lives butt up against difficult or tragic problems. Then we are like the biblical Job, demanding to know why the good suffer and the evil prosper. Usually, when our lives are going well, we are not so deeply concerned with this problem. The religious person will say that we look for God because He has instilled in us an instinct to seek Him. The agnostic will say that looking for an ultimate design is a sign of weakness or immaturity and that the mature person will accept the fact that life is absurd and that no force is in charge.

2. Paragraph 6: "What I got in Sunday-school—besides a wide acquaintance with Christian hymnology—was simply a firm conviction that the Christian faith was full of palpable absurdities, and the Christian God preposterous. "

3. The opposite viewpoint would claim that all of life has a purpose and is moving toward a predestined goal. Allow students to think of aspects of nature that prove predictability. Possible examples: The seasons always follow each other in a predictable sequence of spring, summer, autumn, and winter. After living in the ocean for as long as ten years, salmons will surmount horrendous obstacles in order to return upstream to their hatching sites to spawn. A heavy object thrown from a high window inevitably falls down, not up.

4. Most students will probably show a bias in the way they answer this question. The truth is that many avowed agnostics have faced death with confidence and serenity, but, of course, so have believers. Perhaps the way one copes with the vicissitudes of life is dependent on basic personality as well as philosophical stance.

Cathy Young, *Feminism As. Multiculturalism* (pp. 538-40)

Answers to Questions About the Facts

1. She suggests that the two have opposed philosophies, especially in the treatment of women. For instance, to support all aspects of Indian culture would mean to support the practice of widows burning themselves to death after their husbands die.

2. She was surprised and shocked that the instructor seemed to equate the American male's present discrimination against women with that of the Indian male. She felt that such Indian traditions as killing female newborns or allowing widows to immolate them-

selves could in no way be compared with such American discriminations as losing a job.

3. Cliterodectomy, polygamy, and wife-beating.
4. The example of a Chinese immigrant named Dong Lu Chen, who bludgeoned his wife to death because she had been unfaithful. He was charged with manslaughter and was sentenced to five years probation.
5. The fear that if we become overly protective of foreign cultures and their customs, we might begin to mimic some of their bad customs.

Answers to Questions About Strategies

1. The thesis is found in the final paragraph—giving it a position of finality and power. The opening paragraph and final paragraph are the most emphatic places for key ideas.
2. The author must establish the fact that feminism and multiculturalism are often incompatible, or her final argument—that it is sometimes more important to inculcate Western ideals in immigrants than to uphold their cultural traditions—will not hold.
3. The author is a woman and she uses "I" throughout the essay, giving the argument a highly personal vantage point. She also refers to her own personal experience at a community college.
4. By using the conjunction "similarly" to announce a comparison between paragraphs 6 and 7.
5. The purpose is to get the reader to think. No, the questions are not answered in the essay, but, of course, the reader is to answer them with a convincing "No, we must never condone violence to women!"

Answers to Questions About the Issues

1. Allow students to debate the issue—and especially to share experiences. If immigrants are in the class, they should be encouraged to share their views. We believe that it is possible that some ancestral customs could be debasing to women and where that is the case, human rights must always overrule ancestral customs.
2. Students will enjoy discussing this question. We believe that the customs and traditions of immigrants often enrich our own. For instance, the Chinese reverence for old age, the Japanese admiration for hard work, the Armenian loyalty to their motherland, and the Indian love for spirituality are traditions we might well imitate. Naturally, we deplore traditions of violence, greed, and excessive chauvinism.

3.   If the wrong people attain power, anything is possible; however, we find it difficult to imagine that our society—with its strong emphasis on individual freedom and human rights—could ever revert to admiring such sadistic customs as cliterodectomy, polygamy, immolation, or wife beating. Nevertheless, constant vigilance is required because history teaches us how nations can easily be misguided to espouse tyranny, immorality, and even cruelty.

4.   Allow for students' personal suggestions. (See our examples in the answer to question 2).

5.   Good areas to discuss are the following: equal job opportunities, equal pay, equal responsibility for the children, equal apparel, equal sports training, equal etiquette, etc. You might even discuss such subjects as women bearing arms in the military, women firefighters, women general surgeons, women football players, etc.

Ishmael Reed, America: *The Multinational Society* (pp. 542-46)

Answers to Questions About the Facts

1.   It may seem strange to some readers that Detroit—a city representing America's car industry and considered typically American—should turn out to house large numbers of Islamic as well as Hispanic people.

2.   He is trying to point out the irony of a white Yale professor being the one who is informing a group of serious black American intellectuals about their own heritage.

3.   "Monolithic" means to exhibit massive uniformity, which, he feels, Europe certainly does not since she herself is influenced and shaped by all kinds of forces (review the examples of art, cited at the end of the paragraph).

4.   Because he believes that such an attitude leads to radical thinking expressed in the slogans of hooligans who believe in "White Power" which in its cruel and bigoted arrogance willingly destroys other races it considers inferior.

5.   He insists that while they were "a daring lot," they had a mean streak—punishing people in a cruel and inhuman manner, including exterminating the Indians, who had taught them how to survive.

Answers to Questions About Strategies

1.   It is the opening sentence of paragraph 5. Reed begins his essay with four paragraphs of examples or anecdotes that exemplify or

illustrate his thesis. Often authors place the thesis in the opening or closing paragraph, but Reed chooses to lead up to his thesis by first providing numerous illustrations of his main point.

2. He is reaffirming his admiration and support of blurred cultural styles—that is, the convergence of many cultural aspects into one place. Leaving out the brain metaphor would weaken the paragraph because it supports the point that intellect and emotion must blend to create a truly great nation. Doubtless the name of the visionary politician was withheld so as to avoid any political overtones.

3. To draw attention to the multicultural aspects of one particular quarter—the Lower East Side—in New York. The quotation serves as a microcosm of the larger multicultural tendency of the entire United States.

4. The strategy of causal analysis (demonstrating causes or effects). For instance, at the beginning of paragraph 8, the author states that the term "western civilization" is confusing because its pure origins are being challenged and disputed. In paragraphs 9 and 10, some of our national bigotry is traced back to the Colonial Puritans, who had a mean streak and who exterminated Indians and accused people from the Barbados of being witches. The author also states that the intolerant attitudes of the Puritan Elect—a special group of insiders—continues to have an effect on every-day life in the United States today in the form of a university president belittling the study of African cultures, or a television network boasting that its show of Vatican art represents "the finest achievements of the human spirit."

5. The essay is written from the first person point of view and is filled with personal experiences. The fact that poets call him, that he listens to Yale professors, that he converses with artists, and that he knows a great deal about U.S. as well as international history, gives credibility to the author's argument.

Answers to Questions About the Issues

1. Students need to ponder this question from the point of view of what foreign cultures bring to our country. We believe that the author is correct in his belief that the U.S. is already a nation where the cultures of other nations criss-cross. We also believe that a variety of cultures and traditions is what makes a nation exciting and attractive. Monolithic cultures tend to be regimented, stiff, and unimaginative. Their arts tend to be stagnant and their intellectual lives spiritlessly pedestrian.

2. Certainly, the Puritan literature lends some credence to the fact that the Puritans were narrow-minded in their theological beliefs, that they had an exaggerated sense of sobriety, and that they were often racially prejudiced. Nevertheless, we do not wish to belittle their strong contribution to the democratic way of life and to a social and economic system in which people worked hard and helped each other in times of stress or sorrow.

3. Allow for open discussion. Most colleges in the United States have English as a Second Language programs that provide students with teachers whose specialty is the acquisition of English as a foreign language. We believe, however, that these classes should contain a floor below which students must take classes in high school or adult education, not on a college campus. In other words, to enroll in college, students should test at a certain acceptable level that will allow quickly to move into mainstream courses.

4. If taken to its literal extremes, the term "western civilization" may be a confusing category, but it is nevertheless useful when one deals with historical periods, such as the decline of the Roman Empire and the rise of Western European civilization with its concomitant political, economic, and social institutions that explain our present-day civilization. Such a concept surely helps us to understand present world problems. It also helps us to classify literature, art, music, and other categories.

5. Have students come up with creative ideas that will prevent the kind of strife so common in places like Somalia, the Balkans, Russia, and the Middle East. College campuses have addressed this problem by offering study abroad, courses about the history of foreign cultures, and cultural sensitivity or tolerance workshops.

Chapter Nine ARGUMENTATION

John C. Sherwood *Introduction to Logic* (pp. 561-65)

Answers to Questions About the Facts

1. Answered in paragraph 1: "What really distinguishes the rational from the irrational thinker is not the presence or absence of belief, but the grounds on which belief is accepted. "

2. Answered in paragraph 3. Legitimate sources of belief are evidence and investigation.

3. Also answered in paragraph 3. Induction generalizes, from a number of cases, that a characteristic true of these cases will also be true of other similar cases. Deduction puts ideas together to discover what other ideas can be inferred from them.

4. Answered in paragraph 4. Faith in the uniformity of nature—that the laws of matter will be the same tomorrow as they are today.
5. Answered in paragraph 5. The chief difference is that common sense does not bother to work out the steps leading to its conclusions, while logic does.
6. Answered in paragraph 6. A proposition is a group of words that can be affirmed or denied, of which it can be said that it is either true or false. Propositions are assembled on the basis of evidence or experience. The difference between a proposition and an axiom is that the first can be either proved or disproved, while the second is unprovable.
7. Answered in paragraph 7. A fact can be either proved or disproved; a judgment involves a statement of value. Generalizations differ from judgments in not necessarily implying approval or disapproval. See the example given by the author at the end of paragraph 7.

Answers to Questions About the Strategies

1. The word *belief* is repeated in the opening sentence of the first four paragraphs. Repeating a key term in the opening sentence of a paragraph ensures a smooth transition from one paragraph to the next; it also adds to the coherence of the argument.
2. The use of examples adds precision and clarity to the explanations. You might take this opportunity to point out to students that the lack of concrete examples is responsible for much insipid freshman writing.
3. Primarily on deduction. The author is inferring one idea from another and giving examples to support his conclusions.
4. The use of *we* appeals to the experience of the reader who has no doubt had to draw similar inferences. Its effect is to involve the similar experience of the reader.
5. These are also known as clichés.

Answers to Questions About the Issues

1. Example: *Fact:* "I received an A in my marine biology class. "
   Judgment: "My marine biology class was excellent because it made me more sensitive to the cruelty of fishermen who catch otters to sell them on the fur market." A fact is a verifiable representation of reality; a judgment is a personal value opinion (involving approval or disapproval) that is difficult to verify.
2. Allow for individual responses. Certainly it was good for physicists to abandon past beliefs and accept Einstein's logic that

mass is equivalent to energy. On the other hand, perhaps it was not good to accept the logic of the atomic bomb while abandoning previous beliefs about avoiding inhumane warfare.
3.   Allow for individual responses.
4.   Opinion polls can tell us who is momentarily popular and who is not. But, they have often failed to account for subtle opinions or inexplicable shifts in political atmospheres. For instance, despite the general popularity of the Women's Equal Rights Amendment, it never received enough support to be incorporated into the Constitution. Also, while a majority of people asked will insist that ethnic, religious, or sexual orientation does not influence their vote, the results of voting indicate otherwise.
5.   When the assertion, if acted on, could result in great harm; when it is contrary to common sense; or when it contradicts all of the experts in the field.

Jonathan Swift *A Modest Proposal* (pp. 567-74)

Answers to Questions About the Facts

1.   The chief assumption of this piece is that the children are being consumed by the state in being allowed to starve to death naturally. Swift extends this idea by proposing that since these children are to be consumed and destroyed by a heartless society, then some more useful outlet for their destruction could be found.
2.   The landlords have the best title to the children because they devour their parents through excessive rents. Swift was inveighing against the English absentee landlord.
3.   Swift is saying that society values all life, even the life of children, in economic terms.
4.   There was at that time bitter feeling between Protestant England and Catholic Ireland.
5.   That is what is so devastating about his satire, that it is logical. The children were being destroyed by the heartless neglect of Ireland by the English, and conditions were as heinous as Swift describes them. However, when he logically extends the idea that the children are to be destroyed anyway and therefore some usefulness could be gained from their destruction, Swift is proposing that they substitute systematic destruction for destruction through neglect. His proposal, given the state of things, is entirely logical and utilitarian. The only difference is that it would require the English to openly acknowledge that they were killing children rather than allowing neglect to do it for them.

Answers to Questions About the Strategies

1. The word *modest* is savagely ironic. His proposal is "modest" when compared to the savagery of the conditions the children must suffer. Moreover, it is a savage comment, through the persona, on the insensitivity of man.

2. These are words that cattle breeders would normally use in talking about their animals. These words underscore the terrible conditions of the children; they also characterize the heartlessness of the persona.

3. In paragraph 1 Swift presents a picture of the true state of things; in paragraph 5 he writes about mothers who have abortions or who commit infanticide. Throughout the satire, Swift mingles his proposal with descriptions of how things are. (See paragraph 17.)

4. The tone has variously been described as "savage, " "bitter, " "rancorous. " Swift is considered a satirist after the manner of Juvenal. Juvenalian satire is biting, bitter, and angry.

5. The paragraph gives a savage jab to the nature of man, especially by suggesting that some may believe that the writer's proposal is made for personal gain because he has many children that he could sell under such a scheme.

Answers to Questions About the Issues

1. Throughout history, satire has been effective in drawing attention to social ills. Human beings fear being made a laughing stock for others. Even little children hate being laughed at by their peers or their elders and will discontinue behavior that makes them look absurd—unless they are playing the role of comedians who intend to have the audience laugh with them, not at them. The fact is that Swift became a national hero of the Irish because of this ironically satirical piece, which helped galvanize the Irish people to fight British economic oppression.

2. They are revealed in paragraphs 29-30, where Swift deals with such matters as taxing absentee landlords, using Irish products, being patriotic, having harmony, and working hard and skillfully. Since the entire essay is ironic, what he claims *not* to suggest is exactly what *he* is suggesting.

3. This is an opportunity for students to reflect on social conditions and to come up with creative satirical proposals. Give them free rein to imagine.

4. Allow for varying opinions. We believe that audience determines the style and content of writing. For instance, if one were writing for the Senate of the United States, one would take a straightfor-

ward approach; however, if one were a freelance journalist, writing an editorial for a newspaper, satire would be appropriate.

5. Allow for varying opinions. We believe the essay is still appropriate today because it calls for cohesion, unity, diligence, and compassion within government.

Judy Syfers *I Want A Wife* (pp. 575-77)

Answers to Questions About the Facts

1. She supports the husband while he goes to school, takes care of the children, does all the shopping, and arranges for the babysitting.
2. Answered in paragraph 4. These needs include picking up after the husband, ironing his clothes, cooking his meals, caring for him when he is sick, and taking care of the children on vacation.
3. See paragraph 8. Among other things, she implies that husbands expect their wives to remain faithful while they want to be free to have love affairs. She also accuses husbands of sexual selfishness.
4. See paragraph 6. Numerous, including entertaining guests.

Answers to Questions About the Strategies

1. A large part. Of course, the answers you get will depend on whether or not your students think husbands are as rotten as the author claims. Nevertheless, exaggeration is obviously central to the tone of the writing.
2. It is satirical and sarcastic. An interesting experiment would be to see if your students can identify how the author achieves her sarcastic tone.
3. In fact, she uses no pronoun at all, which is why she keeps repeating "wife" instead of saying "she. " She does this because she is a woman and it might seem ludicrous for her to be longing for another woman as a wife. But a secondary effect of using "wife" rather than a pronoun is to lay the burden of inequity and unfairness not on gender, but on the housewife role, which a man could also play.
4. She uses italics three times, in paragraphs 4, 8, and 11. The first two uses are italicized *my's*, which emphasize the selfishness of husbands. The second is of *wouldn't*, making it clear that anyone would want a wife.

Answers to Questions About the Issues

1. Allow for open discussion. You ought to get a myriad of conflicting answers to this question.
2. Allow for open discussion. The question calls for personal pinion.
3. Allow for open discussion. The question calls for personal opinion. He or she would probably turn out to be a crushing bore.
4. Allow for open discussion.

Andrew Vachss *Sex Predators Can't Be Saved* (pp. 579-82)

Answers to Questions About the Facts

1. The essay deals with sexual violence. It differs fromother crimes in that the criminal cannot be rehabilitated, but will, in most cases, continue his violence, becoming worse as time passes.
2. The immediate cause is lack of empathy on the part of the sex offender. The remote cause is usually physically or emotional abuse in childhood. The sociopathology develops during childhood.
3. Sex offenders choose their violent behavior because, according to the author, while childhood experiences contribute toward the way an adult behaves, they do not force the adult to behave a certain way. Everyone has freedom of choice.
4. Because he enjoys killing and raping.
5. It is completely ineffective, with a high percentage of recidivism regardless of whether the offender was given therapy or not. In some cases, psychiatric therapy made the criminal worse.

Answers to Questions About Strategies

1. The author places it at the very end of his essay—leaving the reader with much to think about. His conclusion is powerful because he states that a life sentence without parole is the only answer to "an epidemic of sexual violence that threatens to pollute our society beyond the possibility of its own rehabilitation." In other words, if we do not do something to stop these violent sex offenders, they may infect our society to the point where it is beyond cure.
2. He cites facts and statistics (paragraph 9).
    He uses his own experience and that of others.
    He uses expert testimony in the form of research documents.
    He takes into account the opposition—people who advocate psychiatric help, castration, appeasement, and rehabilitation.

145

He appeals to the reader's intelligence by using common logic.

3. The point of view—that of a lawyer who has represented many child molestations and other abuse cases in court—is highly effective because the reader is confident that the author speaks from experience and not from fantasy.
4. The reader is warned in the title of the essay.
5. The author uses figurative language to explain rather than to emote, such as when he states, "There's a missing card, one that cannot be put back in the deck once the personality is fully formed" to explain deviant behavior (paragraph 5). Or, when he uses the analogy of a "rock dropped into a calm pool" (paragraph 16) to demonstrate how the problem can grow. Or, when he uses the metaphor of the "osmotic membrane" to suggest the irreversible nature of illness in sex predators (paragraph 18).

Answers to Questions About the Issues

1. Allow students to debate this question openly and frankly. You might ask if religion could have an influence, pointing to such groups as Alcoholics Anonymous, who seem to be successful with their appeal to a Higher Power.
2. The importance of self-esteem is no longer questioned among psychologists or sociologists. When human beings believe themselves to be stupid, evil, or unimportant, their social behavior will reflects this view of self. You might discuss the presence or lack of presence in the story "A Good Man is Hard to Find" by Flannery O'Connor (p.154-66)
3. The process of castrating a human being, while seemingly logical and especially appropriate for sex offenders, contains many dangers (discrimination, wrong identity) and would probably not prevent a hardened sex offender from giving vent to his violence, which is not primarily sexual, but simply uses sex as one tool for venting this violence.
4. Discuss such reasons as the natural desire to try to understand criminals, one's sense of compassion, and perhaps a basic lack of self-esteem that leads to a liking for troubled people.
5. Students should be encouraged not just to accept Vachss' ideas, but to come up with creative ideas of their own. For instance, what about education? What about support groups of their own kinds? What about contributing their talents (when they have some) to the community?

Sylvia Rabiner *How the Superwoman Myth Puts Women Down* (pp. 584-87)

Answers to Questions About the Facts

1. In the old days, a woman was judged a success by the man she had ensnared. If he was a good provider and she kept a good house and had a few decent children, she was judged a success. The author claims that the successful woman today is expected to combine marriage, motherhood, and career.
2. The model of the capitalist feminist—the woman who succeeds executive, wife, and mother.
3. She blames their choice on economics and on uneducated parents who keenly remembered the Depression and did not know how to guide their bright daughters.
4. Because it oppresses them with an unrealistic role model and succeeds only in making most women feel like failures.
5. The irony is that it is an image generated by the success of feminism, which began as a liberation movement for women.

Answers to Questions About the Strategies

1. The central idea of the article is clearly expressed in its title. The author then proceeds to support and document the central idea—that unrealistic female role models are oppressive to women. It is only in the final paragraph that she summarizes what is already long obvious to the reader—that the superwoman image places emphasis on a false ideal of individual success that the vast majority of women cannot live up to. Students need to be told that while most articles have a clearly expressed thesis somewhere in their initial paragraphs, others are organized around a central idea that is understood, though not necessarily formally expressed as a thesis, as in this instance. They also need to be cautioned that only the disciplined writer can stick firmly to an implied, though not expressed, thesis—as this writer does.
2. They provide examples of the superwomen images that the author finds so oppressive.
3. Contrast—she is contrasting the reality of her life as a working mother with the glamorous lives of the superwomen.
4. Part 1—beginning with the first paragraph and ending with the third—introduces the myth of the superwoman and humorously describes the envy it arouses in the author. Part 2—consisting of

paragraphs 4, 5, and 6—gives examples of superwomen as they are portrayed in the media. Part 3—paragraphs 7, 8, and 9—describes the reality of the author's life as a working mother. Part 4, comprising paragraphs 10, 11, and 12, analyzes and discusses the oppressive myth of the superwoman.

5. She uses details about single women who believe they are failing if they can't find a permanent relationship; working mothers who hate to leave their children, and so on. This is a useful example of how once she has made a general statement, the author quickly gets down to cases.

Answers to Questions About the Issues

1. Doubtless Rabiner is right when she states that only a few privileged women can attain the most advanced degrees, be married to top executives whom they adore, have top executive jobs themselves, look utterly elegant, and have well-behaved children. But the truth is that happiness does not lie in status, money, or power; it lies in having close love relationships. It follows, then, that a woman who has experienced the hardships described by Rabiner can still be happy by maintaining hope, by keeping close to her children, and by performing well on the job until she finds a better one. With the right attitude, she might even someday fall in love with a successful man who will encourage her career and with whom she can happily share her life. The editors have found that it never pays to envy anyone else, for we cannot know with certainty what is going on in another person's life. Often what appears so enviable is only a sham.

2. Many people, including women, are strongly opposed to the feminist movement, believing that it has pushed women into careers they never wanted, that it has made the role of homemaker seem lackluster, and that it has given divorced women a bad deal because men no longer pay them enough alimony to let them survive without going to work. A mere half century ago the feminist movement was considered outrageous and led by a strident group of women who hated men.

3. Advantages: higher income, considerable excitement if the career is challenging, the feeling that one is contributing to society, etc. Disadvantages: Difficulty in finding time to rear a family properly, stress on the job, perhaps a sense of competing with one's mate, etc.

4. Allow for individual answers to this question.

5. Allow for individual answers to this question.

James Michie *Dooley Is a Traitor* (pp. 589-92)

Answers to Questions About the Facts

1. His primary objection to war is that it involves coldblooded, passionless killing.
2. The first argument is the patriotic one: right ideas against wrong. The second, an extension of the first, is an appeal to Christianity. The third argument is an attempt to arouse Dooley's emotions, by suggesting that the enemy is threatening him and his family with harm.
3. The judge's arguments are illogical and appeal to emotion.

Answers to Questions About the Strategies

1. The rhyme adds a bounding, humorous effect to the lines.
2. Dooley is characterized as a cockney criminal. The characterization is achieved through his dialogue with the judge. Dooley is made to speak slang, for example, "baccy" for "tobacco," "brainpan" for "mind." Dooley's arguments against killing are given added credence by the fact that he is a murderer.
3. The judge is characterized one-dimensionally as a typical stuffy magistrate. The characterization is achieved, for what it is worth, by his dialogue with Dooley. Clearly the judge is a straw man in this poem.

Answers to Questions About the Issues

1. Have students give their individual evaluations of the saying "All's fair in love and war." Chronicled history and literature offer countless examples of nations wiping out other nations without any moral qualms, and of men and women ruining families and even committing crimes by falling in love with someone to whom they were attracted. As an example of war, consider how the Old Testament Jews mercilessly wiped out the surrounding tribes of Amorites, Amalekites, or Moabites—leaving no one, not even children or cattle. As an example of love, consider the intrigue between Lancelot and Queen Guenevere, which eventually destroyed King Arthur's Round Table. Countless other examples can be cited.
2. Using the persona of a criminal has the advantage of telling the reader something like this: If this toughened jailbird considers it immoral to kill people whom he does not know and against whom

he cannot possibly bear a private grudge, then why should any of us support war efforts in which we kill thousands of people who never did us any personal harm?

3. Allow for differing opinions on this question.

Jo Goodwin Parker *What Is Poverty?* (pp. 594-97)

Answers to Questions About the Facts

1. She feels that the welfare bureaus dehumanized her by making her wait endlessly only to send her to other offices, where she had to repeat her humiliating needs over and over again. She feels like an animal in a herd, being shuttled from place to place without getting any satisfaction. Allow for open discussion on the second question.
2. Soap costs money and hot water costs money; both are necessary to doing laundry.
3. She looks prematurely old because of the hardships she has endured: her back is bent and her hands are cracked.
4. She thinks of her children and how they will suffer if she does not find help.
5. The worst sort of hardnosed citizen, who believes that poverty is the result of laziness or immoral behavior. He is the kind of person who tells the world, "Pull yourself up by your own boot-straps"—even if the person addressed has no bootstraps.

Answers to Questions About the Strategies

1. The entire essay is controlled by the title, "What Is Poverty?" Yes, the strategy is successful because the reader receives a complete and vivid definition of poverty at its most wretched.
2. The most obvious technique is to repeat the word *poverty* at the beginning of most paragraphs.
3. Paragraph 4: "Poverty is dirt. " This is a metaphor to reveal one aspect of poverty. Other figures include "Poverty is asking for help" and "Poverty is remembering." These are figures of speech to define poverty; they are not lexical definitions.
    Paragraph 10: "black future" is a metaphor for hopelessness.
    Paragraph 14: "when asking for help does not eat away the last bit of pride" is a personification of the pain sustained as a result of lost pride.
4. Allow discussion on this point. Students should find the conclusion effective because of its restrained pathos. The author is not begging for sympathy for herself but for all others who suffer her plight. The anger she wants us to feel is anger for the fact that society

allows this kind of poverty to exist. The conclusion is simple but powerful.

5. One might use a lexical definition: "Poverty is the condition of being unable to provide the most necessary material needs or comforts."

Answers to Questions About the Issues

1. Students might disagree on what aspect is the worst, but certainly Parker's claim of looking into "a black future" makes her despair palpable. One can endure almost anything when there is hope, but when hope dies, the human spirit is forced to struggle beyond its normal capacity to survive.
2. Here is an opportunity for students to relate their own experience in such bureaus as the Department of Motor Vehicles, Of Office of Unemployment, and offices in City Hall. Compare these agencies with your physician or attorney's offices.
3. Since this essay was published in 1971, much has been done for the poor, but much more needs to be done. Women, in particular, have received help through better government subsidies for food and living accommodations; yet, much more needs to be done. While generous food stamp programs are available, and unemployment benefits can be claimed by those who have paid into social security, there are still thousands of poor who live out on the streets, in parks, or under bridges. Homeless women and men wander the main streets of our major cities, lacking proper food or medical treatment. Poverty is still one of our major problems.
4. We are given no specific reasons for the divorce. However, the author blames herself and having so many children. She seems to take the divorce for granted and does not blame the husband, but hopes he improved his lot since leaving her, for he could not do so while she and the children were there to drag him down. Have your students discuss the moral implications of what the husband did by leaving this woman to care for four children while she had no education or skills to take on the task.
5. Social studies indicate that when the poor have nothing more to lose, they will turn to revolutions or crime for help. Unless someone reaches these people with a hand that offers spiritual as well as material help, most of them are destined to end in the county hospital or in prison because decency and morality offer them nothing they desperately need. The immediate solution is to have society provide a safe environment and enough food for everyone—even if it means paying higher taxes.

Joseph Perkins, *Homeless: Expose the Myths* (p. 599-600)

Answers to Questions About the Facts

1. He spent a night near Grand Central Station, a favorite gathering place for the homeless of New York City. This way he could observe first hand who the homeless were and why they were on the streets.
2. The author discovered right away that the homeless were not middle class or average people who had fallen on hard times. They were, in fact, people suffering from mental illness or from substance abuse.
3. Their insistence that homelessness and poverty are an economic problem to which we can supply economic answers, such as spending more money on creating homes and jobs for these unfortunates.
4. Two events occurred: All but the most dangerous patients were dismissed from state mental hospitals, and drug use exploded.
5. Pay more attention to their mental problems and their self-destructive substance abuse.

Answers to Questions About the Strategies

1. Despite its brevity, the essay is convincing because all of us have observed homeless street people in our large cities, and most of them fall into the two categories mentioned by Perkins. Some of us have also observed what might be considered con artists who have a professional talent for begging.
2. To draw attention to the fact that we do not really want (or know how) to help the homeless. The author could have ended as follows: "We should help the homeless by paying more attention to their mental health and substance abuse problems."
3. He uses the pronoun "This" at the beginning of paragraph 11 to refer back to the content of paragraph 10.
4. "Myths" in the author's sense refers to a set of false assumptions that pervade society's thinking, such as the myth that the homeless are really just normal, average people who have fallen on bad times, but who could be off the streets if they were given jobs and affordable housing.
5. It is simple and straightforward, without poetic imagery or fanciful language. It is journalistic writing at its most effective because it does not waste the reader's time, but gets straight to the point.

Answers to Questions About the Issues

1. Hoboes are colorful, romantic characters who hop trains and travel from place to place, having chosen a life of independent adventure over a life of regularity and complacency. Bums are men who are too lazy to work regularly, being content to live off the generosity of give-away plans or handouts. Today's homeless are different from hoboes and bums in that the homeless are mentally ill whereas the traditional hoboes and bums were not.

2. Economic policies can certainly influence the amount of capital people amass and the amount of profit they make, but family life and education are far more important than economic policies when it comes to people's mental health.

3. The most compelling support is found in paragraph 11, where we are told that a survey conducted by the U.S. Conference of Mayors found that 28 percent of the homeless population in the cities were mentally ill and 41 percent substance abusers. One cannot deny these statistics.

4. Both positions have value. Certainly creating jobs for people who need them, feeding the hungry, and providing affordable housing for the disadvantaged are programs with considerable merit. However, providing mentally ill people with hospital stay and psychiatric care is also admirable. Perhaps we need to balance liberalism with conservatism when it comes to the needy.

5. The question should motivate students to come up with some creative ideas. For instance, there was a time during the Depression of the 1920's when certain people in Southern California pitched tents and lived in state parks because they had lost their houses. They told stories of warmth and even fun in these tent communities.

Chapter Ten THE MEANING OF WORDS

George Orwell *Politics and the English Language* (pp. 611-22)

Answers to Questions About the Facts

1. Orwell takes the position that bad writing habits lead to muddled thinking, which reinforces whatever degenerate politics already exist. According to him, the process becomes a vicious circle: language becomes "ugly and inaccurate because our thoughts are

foolish, but the slovenliness of our language makes it easier for us to have foolish thoughts." (See paragraph 2.)
2. Staleness of imagery and lack of precision.
3. People use hackneyed imagery and prefabricated phrases because it takes less effort to reel them out than to think of original ways of expressing themselves. (See paragraph 12.)
4. Foreign words, according to Orwell, usually increase the slovenliness and vagueness of the writer's language. (See the last sentence of paragraph 7.) Have your students suggest some foreign words that they tend to use in writing. Examples: *objets d'art, ambiance, mea culpa, weltschmerz, de facto, carpe diem, c'est la vie, detente.*
5. Orwell means that much political writing attempts to persuade people that the government is doing what is morally right, when in actuality it is committing acts of plunder, robbery, and torture against innocent people. He says, "When there is a gap between one's real and one's declared aims, one turns as it were instinctively to long words and exhausted idioms, like a cuttlefish squirting out ink" (paragraph 15). A good class project is to collect samples of euphemisms from contemporary politics.
6. Orwell believes the meaning should dictate the word, not the other way around. This is best accomplished through pictures and sensations. Instead of writing "It is cold outside," one might write "The wind is howling like a wounded animal and icicles are hanging from the rain gutters. "
7. Reread the rules listed in paragraph 18. Other rules might come to mind, but rule (vi) probably covers them.

Answers to Questions About the Strategies

1. Examples of fresh imagery:
    Paragraph 1:   "It follows that any struggle against the abuse of language is a sentimental archaism, like preferring candles to electric light or hansom cabs to aeroplanes."
    Paragraph 4:   ". . . phrases tacked together like the sections of a prefabricated henhouse."
    Paragraph 5:   "But in between these two classes there is a huge dump of wornout metaphors. . . . "
    Paragraph 12:   "It consists in gumming together long strips of words which have already been set in order by someone else,. . ."
    Paragraph 12:   "In (4), the writer knows more or less what he wants to say, but an accumulation of stale phrases chokes him like tea leaves blocking a sink."

2. Orwell compares the relationship between muddled thinking and muddled writing to the cause-effect relationship of an alcoholic's sense of failure and his excessive drinking. The more the alcoholic feels himself to be a failure, the more he drinks, and the more he drinks, the more he feels himself to be a failure.
3. Paragraph 5.
4. The transition is made in the last sentence of paragraph 12: "It is at this point that the special connection between politics and the debasement of language becomes clear."
5. The topic sentence is "In our time, political speech and writing are largely the defence of the indefensible." The paragraph is developed through examples.

Answers to Questions About the Issues

1. The editors do not consider American English to be in a bad way. True, much of the general populace writes poorly, using trite language and revealing a complete lack of knowledge of grammatical structure. This flaw is to be expected in a country that continues to absorb hundreds of thousands of immigrants into its social structure. Nevertheless, our vast publishing trade—consisting of excellent daily newspaper editorials, well turned fiction, striking poetry, and a variety of other kinds of good writing—is ample proof of the fact that we have talented and accomplished writers to model after. As long as this situation prevails, we need not descend into Orwell's despair about English.
2. Have students mull over this question. One example the editors have often encountered is freshman compositions that have been hastily and thoughtlessly dashed onto a page. When these are then read aloud in class, the authors are overcome with embarrassment at how foolish they sound.
3. Have students suggest some metaphors they often hear. To get them started, here are three examples: (1) "I'm bored out of my skull in Mr. Smith's class"; (2) "Prime Minister Thatcher is a tough cookie"; (3) "Our country must give birth to some new attitudes."
4. Suggest that students look through cheap magazines, political speeches, or even textbooks in technology. Some students might even be brave enough to bring samples of their own writing.
5. Students should be encouraged to focus on those faults mentioned by Orwell that they most clearly see in their own writing.

Robin Lakoff *You Are What You Say* (pp. 623-29)

Answers to Questions About the Facts

1. The opening sentence of the essay defines "women's language" as "that pleasant (dainty?), euphemistic, never-aggressive way of talking we learned as little girls. " It is important that this definition be given from the start of the essay so that the reader knows the author's point of view. Many of us feel that the definition no longer holds in professional circles, insisting that women's language has moved away from that definition and from the definition of being a conveyor of gossip. For women holding such jobs as college professors, lawyers, physicians, or engineers, their language will probably not vary much from that of men in those same jobs.

2. The author states that these colors require fine distinctions that are more relevant to a woman's vocabulary—presumably because women are often in charge of decorating the interior of homes and tend to wear more colorful clothing than men. Have students offer their own opinions on whether or not males see colors differently than women do.

3. The reason offered is that women don't want to sound aggressive or opinionated. It seems to us that in this case the author may be too harsh on women when she accuses them of using tag questions because they are unsure of themselves or do not wish to commit themselves to a definite statement. Perhaps women just like to be polite, allowing for the possibility that the person addressed may have a different opinion. By not being dogmatic, the woman encourages the addressee to offer an alternate suggestion without having to feel that he or she is starting a dispute. We feel that men do this too.

4. *Lady* connotes frivolity and exaltation without power; on the other hand, *woman* connotes pure sexuality. Allow for individual opinions on what the students wish the two terms to mean. Consider the following phrases or sentences:
   the girls in the office
   the women on the Board
   the woman in charge of the task force
   the girl at the front desk
   Women should not be priests.
   Girls should not play football.

5. Because they are supposed to be childlike and enjoy such terms. Lately, however, it has become dangerous to use them because women are beginning to lodge sexual harassment suits against men who call them "sweetie," "honey," "babe," or in any other way treat

them like sexual objects. Certain firms have created formal guidelines for the way men treat women in the work place. It has become illegal to treat them as sex objects.

Answers to Questions About the Strategies

1. She uses many, many examples--a crucial kind of evidence because it allows the reader to see exactly what kinds of words are used by and about women. The reader can then judge whether these words really do affect the position women hold in society.
2. The essay is divided into three parts: 1) Paragraphs 1-3: the introduction defining "women's language," 2) Paragraphs 4-18: language used by women, 3) Paragraphs 19-38: language used to describe women. Although no headings or numbering system is used, students should be able to follow the organization because the author introduces each section.
3. The pronoun *this* at the start of paragraph 9 clearly refers back to the tag question "The situation in Southeast Asia is terrible, isn't it?" in paragraph 8.
4. The purpose is to convince women to speak up against words or sentence patterns that make them seem trivial, stupid, or helpless. It is stated explicitly in the final sentence of the essay: "In more ways than one, it's time to speak up. " This is a call for action on the part of the reader.
5. The essay is aimed at an educated audience because the vocabulary is sophisticated, the approach is scholarly, and the subject matter assumes some psychological insight on the part of the reader. We suggest that college students make an ideal reading audience for this essay.

Answers to Questions About the Issues

1. Allow for open discussion on this question. The discussion should focus on whether women are perceived as more timid, trivial, and helpless than men. Perhaps students will suggest some entirely different traits. Some of our male students have suggested that many "modern" women try to emasculate or manipulate men. Throw that idea into the discussion and see where it goes.
2. Tag questions are useful in any situation where the potential for anger exists. For instance, a male who feels attacked by some other male's accusation might forestall a fight by saying, "Jim, you've gone a little too far, don't you think?" rather than, "Jim, you've gone too far." Or, an employer might cause his employee to increase his work speed if he says, "It seems to me you could work just a little

faster, couldn't you, Mike?" That approach would certainly cause less devastation in the employee than if he said, "Look here, Mike, you've got to work faster."

3. In formal situations (especially in a business environment), the term "lady" is rarely used because of exactly what Lakoff has pointed out—the term has acquired a bad connotation of making women seem weak and prissy. Some women complain that they wish men still used the term and they feel rather nostalgic as they reminisce about times when men truly treated women like "ladies."

4. Indeed, the attitude has changed perceptibly. Many women alive today remember well how in their social circles any female was pitied as an "old maid" if she was not married by the age of twenty-five. It seems a healthy and welcome improvement to have society not bat an eye when a woman turns thirty without ever having been married.

5. You can make sure that your own language is free from terms and word patterns that denigrate women and trivialize them. Have students suggest linguistic expressions that should be avoided.

Laura Bohannan *Shakespeare in the Bush* (pp. 632-41)

Answers to Questions About the Facts

1. Bohannan makes the point that culture colors peoples' understanding of words.

2. Examples of customs:
   a. protocol of passing the calabash
   b. receipts for brides
   c. letter writers and readers for hire
   d. chiefs with many wives
   e. peace offerings given to end or avert a quarrel
   f. love of festivities

Examples of beliefs:
   a. Omens are significant.
   b. The dead do not haunt us.
   c. Money is more important than sex.
   d. Madness is the result of witchcraft.
   e. The leaders of the tribe are omniscient.

3. The Tiv begin with "Not yesterday, not yesterday." We begin with "Once upon a time."

4. The breakdown is always caused by different cultural attitudes that in turn cause different interpretations of the incidents in *Hamlet*.

5. The desire to be thought wise and knowledgeable.

158

Answers to Questions about the Strategies

1. The long introduction describes to the reader the primitive setting in which the story is told.
2. Dialogue is used to give the reader a sense of being at the scene of action. It also adds dramatic intensity.
3. The Tiv have no formal academic training. They learn from their forebears and from experience rather than from books.
4. Various answers are possible. Example: "a place where crowds can go to eat food prepared by chief cooks. "
5. Primitive people have their own wisdom and knowledge. We can learn from them.
6. College anthropology majors and other students with a college-level vocabulary will enjoy this article.

Answers to Questions About the Issues

1. The story could be made comprehensible by someone thoroughly versed in the Tiv's customs and beliefs, but it would be considerably adapted from the original Shakespearean version.
2. One might say that certain universal truths seem accepted by all thinking human beings, no matter how sophisticated or primitive. For instance, all cultures promote a code of gratitude for the hand that feeds you; all cultures promote respect for family or tribe; all cultures punish crimes like theft and unprovoked murder. Thus, if we were to tell our stories in terms of these great general truths, they might be understood. Nonetheless, most stories contain the underlying assumptions and customs of the country from which they originated, and these can be extremely complex in advanced civilizations.
3. Cultures with oral story-telling traditions often spawn excellent writers as their civilizations advance. Good examples are the Jews of the Old Testament, the ancient Greeks, and the Irish. Telling stories sharpens one's use of plot, image, and dialogue.
4. Have volunteers pretend that the class is made up of first graders to whom they explain what a ghost is.
5. Allow students to name their choice. Probably the story of David and Goliath could be most easily interpreted since it deals simply with a young boy who, through courage and help from a deity, kills a strong enemy. Most cultures would understand the dynamics involved.

159

Jimmy Santiago Baca, *Coming Into Language* (p.642-49)

Answers to Questions About the Facts

1. He dropped out of school because his teachers had scolded him for not knowing his lessons, making him feel ashamed and afraid.
2. He refused to explain a deep cut on his forearm.
3. William Wordsworth and Samuel Taylor Coleridge are two poets of the Romantic Age in England. Baca finds them in an anthology he stole from one of his guards in the county jail.
4. The island of writing: "I felt an island rising beneath my feet like the back of a whale. As more and more words emerged, I could finally rest: I had a place to stand for the first time in my life."
5. Evidently he had been so heavily medicated during his mental and emotional spells that he was mute and paralyzed.

Answers to Questions About the Strategies

1. The voice is one of intimate sharing, as if the writer were confiding in a journal. It is the voice of a prison inmate who has moved from despair to hope, from hellish torture to hopeful acceptance. Have students share how they felt about the narrator. Did they like him and admire him, or were they turned off by his criminal past?
2. Here is a possible sequence; other possibilities exist, depending on how the steps are discerned:
   1) The author finds and peruses a hospital book with illustrations of the female anatomy.
   2) The author looks at *450 Years of Chicano History*, an illustrated book about Chicano revolts.
   3) The author listens as male prisoners read aloud the works of famous writers.
   4) The author reads a stolen university literature anthology that includes Wordsworth and Coleridge.
   5) The author acquires a Red Chief notebook and starts to write down his impressions of life.
   6) The author finds freedom in language (see paragraph 17).
   7) The author establishes a barter business while in solitary confinement—trading his poems or letters for novels, pencils, and writing tablets.
   8) The author keeps a journal and finds unity with the universe, but also insanity.
   9) The author is moved to death-row and then to the row for mentally-disturbed prisoners.

10) The author emerges from a state of total madness and rejection to be born a poet.

3. Examples abound. Here are three: *Paragraph 5:* "Listening to the words of these writers, I felt that invisible threat from without lessen--my sense of teetering on a rotting plank over swamp water where famished alligators clapped their horny snouts for my blood." *Paragraph 11:* "But soon the heartache of having missed so much of life, that had numbed me since I was a child, gave way, as if a grave illness lifted itself from me and I was cured, innocently believing in the beauty of life again." *Paragraph 17:* "Each word steamed with the hot lava juices of my primordial making, and I crawled out of stanzas dripping with birth-blood, reborn and freed from the chaos of my life."

4. With phrases such as these: "One night. . ." (paragraph 2); "Before I was eighteen. . ." (paragraph 5); Two years passed." (paragraph 8); "One night in my third month in the county jail. . ." (paragraph 9); Days later. . ." (paragraph 23)); "When I had been in the county jail longer than anyone else. . ." (paragraph 18); "After that interview. . ." (paragraph 20); "As the months passed. . ." (paragraph 26).

5. He felt intellectually and socially so inadequate that any question by a stranger or outsider made him feel endangered, as if those questioning him were trying to trap and hang him.

Answers to Questions About the Issues

1. Answers may differ, but certainly paragraph 17 expresses the author's recognition of how language can set one free to experience emotions and to head toward an understanding of the cosmos. He uses the metaphor of the child in a dark room switching on the light.

2. Evidently he had an innate love of syntax and of sentence structure. In fact, twice in the essay he expresses a desire to learn grammar (See paragraphs 12 and 20).

3. The essence of his past was rage, hopelessness, and a sense of betrayal as well as injustice. He was psychologically and spiritually mutilated. What allowed him to become a writer despite his mutilation was his indomitable love for life. As he puts it, he wanted to affirm "breath and laughter and the abiding innocence of things" (see final paragraph).

4. The teaching strategy of humiliating students by having them sit in a corner wearing a dunce cap, by having them wear a sign stating, "I did not study my lesson," or, as the author had to do, by having them stick their noses in a chalk circle on the blackboard, was popular fifty years ago, but has since then come out of favor because it

was found to be poor pedagogy and harmful to students' sense of self and to their future success. The trend today is to build a student's self-confidence, not to tear it down.

5. This question gets to the heart of how prisoners should be treated. We believe that all human beings should live up to their potential talents. A practical approach would be to test prisoners for their abilities and also for their inclinations. Having prisoners attend classes would surely do no harm and might do a great deal of good.

Carl Sandburg *Threes* (pp. 650-51)

Answers to Questions About the Facts

1. Ultimately, the only things in life with real meaning are food, money, and sex.
     Or
   Values change as people grow older.
     Or
   As people age, they become less idealistic and more cynical.
2. Various answers are possible.
3. First: youth and idealism Second: middle age and material security Third: old age and metaphysical security Fourth: deprivation and revolution Fifth: cynicism and personal fulfillment
4. The marine appears to be tough, realistic, and concerned with immediate biological satisfactions.

Answers to Questions About the Strategies

1. The speaker is the poet posing as an omniscient observer.
2. Mustaches, sideburns, and lilacs connote elegance, polish, and success.
3. The juxtaposition stresses how life consists not only of earth-shattering events but also of common, ordinary happenings.
4. The allusion is a reference to the Bolshevik Revolution of 1917, based on the theories of Karl Marx and Friedrich Engles, who asked the workers of the world to unite and take over political leadership because they deserved a decent living wage instead of continuing to be slaves to capitalism.
5. The passing of time is indicated by the symbol of a clock ticking away toward doom and damnation.

1. *Liberté, Egalité, Fraternité* became the watchwords of the Jacobins, a group of radical leaders in 1789 at the start of the French Revolution, when the commoners demanded some of the power to which their new economic position entitled them. It is this revolution that resulted in the execution by guillotine of Louis XVI and his wife, Marie Antoinette.
2. There is no unequivocal answer to this question. Doubtless some people become more idealistic and some more cynical. Perhaps those with a strong belief in the Christian religion become more God-centered and therefore more idealistic, whereas those with a purely materialistic approach to life become more stoic and cynical as they are forced to accept the inevitability and permanence of decay.
3. When the Bolsheviks toppled the czar and established the Communist regime of 1918, they promised the starving peasantry and proletariat permanent access to bread, peace, and land. In the process, millions of people were killed or sent to labor camps to starve to death. Perhaps that is why the syllables are called "dusky," meaning dark and gloomy. The editors are convinced that even today some aspects of the communist plan are still dusky in the sense that human rights continue to be suppressed and therefore the gloom continues.
4. It points out that words have the power to incite war, love, and religion.

Anna Quindlen, *The Great White Myth* (p.653-55)

Answers to Questions About the Facts

1. He wants to know what the future can hold for him when most of the good jobs are going to women and to blacks.
2. Their bitterness is caused by their belief that the process of affirmative action is systematically oppressing white males.
3. Three percent.
4. No; if you actually visit these areas, you find that African Americans do not dominate the job market.
5. The new myth is that the world is full of incompetent black Americans prospering unfairly at the expense of the competent white. The reality is that incompetent white co-workers exist as well.

Answers to Questions About the Strategies

1. Quindlen is a journalist whose style is crisp, uncomplicated, and to the point. Her paragraphs are short so that a busy person can get the gist of it quickly. This journalistic style is commonly used in newspapers and popular periodicals.
2. The repetition creates balance and emphasis. This kind of parallelism is also easy on the ears because it is rhythmic.
3. Its brevity draws attention to its meaning—which is to contradict flatly the contention by some that most construction sites, precinct houses, and investment banks are filled with African Americans.
4. In paragraph 6, when she uses the simile of the hot air balloons and the metaphor of the "blue sky of the American landscape" and "gaudy stripes of hyperbole." The figurative language not only adds sparkle to the paragraph but also it explains what the effect of such exaggeration is on the public.
5. It is stated in the final paragraph as the conclusion to all of the observations made in the earlier paragraphs.

Answers to Questions About the Issues

1. If one were to take a poll of world opinion, doubtlessly the United States would be considered a country highly committed to the individual rights of its citizens. The various laws connected with affirmative action—beginning with the Fourteenth Amendment guaranteeing blacks their civil rights—indicate America's devotion to concrete steps that would encourage employers and educational institutions to make up for past inequities in the work place and in schools. No longer are managers or administrators able to advertise informally through word of mouth, but must insure that all applicants seeking admission to work or school receive the same information. Additionally, affirmative action policies also stopped the practice of discriminating against women in general and pregnant women in particular. In brief, America has made large strides in stopping discrimination.
2. Students should have an interesting debate on this subject. Reasons to hate might include a resentment for religious dogmatism; for lack of high standards of morality, including sexual habits; for having to pay taxes to support irresponsible citizens who refuse to work; and other situations, political, economic, and social.
3. The answer to this question is "yes," because numerous liberal political leaders have indicated that when affirmative action leads to quotas, then it can become racially hostile. In fact, the Supreme

Court itself was split on the issue of whether or not to deny admission to medical school to a white student who had been denied admission in favor of black students less qualified than he.

4.   Students need to think through this question and answer it with a view toward justice, fairness, and long-term harmony among citizens.
5.   Here again, students must think in terms of Plato's Golden Rule. They must imagine that any laws they support will be applied to everyone. Would the law be equally fair to all?

Wilma J. Moore, *The Route to 9066* (pp. 657-60)

Answers to Questions About the Facts

1.   Filling out an application form so her grandson could attend a private elementary school.
2.   1) Understanding of various cultures, 2) wishing to right past wrongs, 3) eliminating racial prejudice.
3.   Because she has observed that the offspring of Russians, Indians, or Japanese have integrated into what we call "American life." They eat American food, listen to American music, and attend American churches.
4.   To Executive Order 9066, which revoked the civil liberties of Japanese Americans.
5.   They both justified their actions as necessary in order to preserve justice and democracy in the United States—based on the erroneous assumption that racial castes are predestined.

Answers to Questions About the Strategies

1.   It presumes a knowledge of what "9066" means. This presumption is probably not warranted because most students may have forgotten the segment of their U.S. history class that explained the 1942 Executive Order 9066, placing Japanese Americans in relocation camps.
2.   A good argument always takes into account the opposition so that it can annihilate it. For instance, a political speech will state, "Now my opponent will insist that. . . . ." And then the speaker will show where the opponent is dead wrong.
3.   She uses repetition ("Today. . . .Tomorrow"). First all, this kind of repetition emphasizes the point that what may be good today may be dangerous tomorrow. Second, the repetition achieves a kind of rhythm that helps the reader assimilate the meaning of the

paragraph. Third, the repetition creates coherence through parallelism.

4. This woman's writing style is logical and erudite. She has obviously read voraciously and thought deeply about her reading. She completely shatters the stereotype of the housewife who in her spare time watches television and gossips with neighbors.

5. Many re-phrasings are possible. Here is an example: "We had better think twice before we continue to follow strict affirmative action guidelines in our schools, lest we end up creating racism rather than avoiding it."

Answers to Questions About the Issues

1. They disagree on their major premises. Quindlen believes that racial discrimination of the past must be righted now by giving minorities certain advantages. She insists that affirmative action is the only way to racial balance. Moore, on the other hand, believes that giving minorities advantages based on their race proclaims to the world that minorities cannot change because they have inborn cultural characteristics. She believes this is a dangerous route that could lead to despotism.

2. Allow students to state their preference spontaneously, but insist that they provide reasons for their preference.

3. The mood was enormous fear, and fear produces irrational decisions.

4. Such an idea is patent nonsense. In one single generation, thousands of immigrants have assimilated perfectly into the American way of life—including speaking perfect English, choosing American foods, loving American music, and making close friends of American associates.

5. Many recipients see affirmative action as a historical necessity in order to keep powerful institutions from categorizing by race; whereas other recipients admit to a feeling of embarrassment and wondering if they really earned the right to be where they are.